# Ready to Go
# Missions

# 12 Complete Plans for Life-Changing Experiences

06 07 08 09 10 11 12 13 14 15– 10 9 8 7 6 5 4 3 2 1

MANUFACTURED IN THE UNITED STATES OF AMERICA

**Development Editor:** Jennifer A. Youngman
**Design Manager:** Keely Moore
**Production Editor:** Susan Heinemann

At the time of publication, all website addresses were correct and operational.

**Designer:** Keely Moore
**Cover Design:** Keely Moore

# Dedication

This book is dedicated first and foremost to God, a faithful God who always provides a way for me to be involved and included in missions even when money is tight. I thank God for introducing me to the world of missions and the blessings in serving others. God has given me strength through the trying times of unique food, less-than-comfortable conditions, bugs, and long days of hard work. Thank you, God, for being there as I grew in my understanding of your call.

Secondly, this book is dedicated to Rev. Fred Baum, who provided opportunities for me as a youth to be in missions and helped teach me the importance of serving others; to my parents, James and Constance; my grandparents, James, Ruth, Ivan, and Irlanda; my uncle John, and other family members who supported my mission trips, always finding a way to contribute a few dollars; to the example of the members of Pender United Methodist Church in Fairfax, Virginia, who live God's call to serve through missions; and to all of the youth who have trusted God and allowed me to lead them in missions. I hope that the wisdom and experience I've been allotted will help encourage others to say, "Here I am Lord; send me," as they embrace God's call.

Finally, this book is dedicated to Laura, Sierra, and Camille. Thank you for the joy that comes with being a husband and father. I see the energy in my two little girls and look forward to the day when they are old enough to understand God's call to serve in love, and for the day when they embrace that call by making missions an important part of their lives.

—Jason

# About the Writer

Originally from Mesa, Arizona, Jason Schultz began his ministry in 1990 as a huddle coach with Fellowship of Christian Athletes and started working with The United Methodist Church in 1992. During his twelve years as a youth minister, He has served churches in Virginia, Tennessee, Washington, and Idaho. Jason lives with his wife, Laura, and his two daughters, Camille and Sierra, in Boise Idaho, where he is Youth Minister at Boise First United Methodist Church, The Cathedral of the Rockies. He has a Bachelor of Arts degree from the University of Washington, Tacoma, where he studied arts, media, and culture. The writer of *Marking Milestones and Making Memories for Youth,* Jason has written for *Combos for Youth Groups,* Volumes 3 and 4, and *The Amazing Bible Race.*

# Contents

# Ready to Go

# Missions: an Overview

So, you want to go on a mission trip but don't have any experience with missions. Perhaps the prospect of taking youth across country—yet alone across town—sounds like as much fun as a root canal. (Actually, a root canal might be less painful because of the anesthetic.)

Well, don't fear; youth mission trips aren't as intimidating as you might think. And my goal in this book is to resource groups interested in doing their first mission trip, as well as seasoned groups looking for new ideas.

In the following pages, you'll find twelve ready-to-go mission opportunities and everything you need to guide youth through the life-changing experiences of serving others. Six of the mission ideas are designed for one- to three-day, shorter-term experiences; six ideas are designed for five days or longer. You can skip right to the ideas now or, if you want to understand missions and mission trip planning in a larger context, continue reading.

Are you ready to change some lives?

## MISSIONS: WHY?

The short answer is because God calls us to do so. Jesus said in the Great Commission, "Therefore go and make disciples of all nations, baptizing them in the name of the Father, Son and Holy Spirit, and teaching them to obey everything I have commanded you" (**Matthew 28:19-20**). Following Christ means loving and serving others, putting them first. It means caring for "the least of these" (**Matthew 25:40**) as Jesus instructs.

The slightly longer answer to "Why do we do missions?" is that we want to love and honor God. And when our group is doing what God calls us to do, we grow closer to one another and partner with God in transforming the world and bringing God's kingdom. Think of your group right now. Are you a circle that faces inward at one another, or a circle that faces outward toward the world?

## MISSION: WHAT?

The purpose of a mission is to serve others in love, facilitate growth in the body of Christ, and transform the world, making it the place God intended. We can do so through words (including preaching and testimonies) and actions (including everyday behavior and putting others before oneself).

A mission benefits others, especially if you are doing a building project or providing a service such as clean-up, vacation Bible school, or classes. But a mission should affect each person participating in the project. Youth often gain as much, if not more, than those they serve. The biggest mistake you can make when planning a mission trip is to have a "we're going to fix them" or "they need our help and we're going to rescue them" approach. Instead, participants should humble themselves and open themselves to what God has to teach them through the experience. Nothing will bring your group closer. The Holy Spirit does amazing things in groups that are serious about missions.

By serving others, youth learn to sacrifice time, energy, some of the basic comforts of life (such as a soft bed and familiar food), and money. Most of us in America live a privileged life with means above the world's standard of living. A mission trip allows youth to experience conditions that much of the world deals with on a daily basis.

Our youth also learn that their preconceived notions about regions or people aren't necessarily accurate. For instance, teens may realize that the people being served aren't "just lazy" but have real barriers and obstacles to deal with. As a result of this experience, youth will discover a selflessness that comes with loving others. This attitude may be countercultural; but one person at a time, it can transform the world.

## MISSION: HOW?

This subject has been the source of some intense . . . um . . . discussions, to say the least. They usually center on construction versus evangelism: "Should our mission trip focus on building a new house, school, or church—or should we focus on preaching the gospel by doing street-drama ministry or vacation

Bible school?" The truth is that God works in both a construction-focused mission trip and an evangelism-focused mission trip. And true missions meet both physical and spiritual needs, so try not to lodge yourself on only one side of the argument. Remember though, that the work of conversion is not ours but belongs to the Holy Spirit; whether or not we hear people pray a conversion prayer, the Spirit works—even after we return home. Remind your youth that the way they act can help preach their message, whether they're on top of a roof nailing down tar paper or standing on a street corner and telling people about Jesus.

## MISSION: WHEN?

There are two approaches to this question: What time of year? and, When is our group ready? Let's start with the latter. There's no magic number your group size has to reach or a measured faith level that everyone must obtain before going on a mission trip. God will use any number of people; and all of the teens, if they're willing, will grow on their faith journey. So take that first trip even if only one or two youth go—they'll come back changed, excited, and willing to recruit more youth to go on the next one.

As for the time of the year, consider a few things such as the weather at the mission site, school schedules, the length of your trip, and the availability of resources. A mission trip to Arizona sounds fun, but the 110-plus-degree temperatures in July are hot, to say the least. An outdoor construction project in Thailand would prove more difficult during monsoon season. Alaska during Christmas break is going to present some issues, with cold and lack of sunlight. Remember that in the southern hemisphere of the earth, seasons are opposite of those in the northern hemisphere. If you're planning to incorporate a fun day that includes white-water rafting, you want to go in spring, when the runoff is high, not September, when rivers are too low for rafting.

Of course, you can't avoid all of these environmental challenges completely; just consider them in determining when to take a trip. You don't want to be like Clark Griswold, who, in *National Lampoon's Vacation,* drives his family from Chicago to California, only to discover that Wally World is closed for maintenance. Do your homework.

Typical times for mission trips are during summer break, Christmas or winter breaks, spring break, Thanksgiving weekend, or other long holiday weekends. If your youth attend various schools, check each school's schedule for corresponding time off; many districts have overlapping breaks. If your youth attend school year-round, as is becoming more popular, summer may not work best for your group.

## MISSION: WHERE?

Are you going to do a local outreach or service project, or a big trip far from home? When determining a project and destination, consider the size of your group, possible travel arrangements, and expenses. Ask yourself also whether the motivation for going is because God is leading or because the location offers great surfing. (Mission: Aloha, anyone?)

Don't overdo things. A trip to Africa sounds sound wonderful, but can your group afford the $3,000-per-person airfare? And are your kids prepared for international travel? Try starting with something that better fits your group, and build up to Africa. Getting to this point may take a few years, but don't worry about it; a local outreach is just as significant and life-changing as a trip to a foreign country.

Eventually, you'll want to look a year or two down the road. So if you think you want to do a more expensive trip in a year or two, you can do a couple of less expensive trips leading up to or following the bigger trip. Some groups work on an every-other-year or every-third-year schedule and alternate doing each type of mission. (Remember that the terms *bigger* and *smaller* refer to the amount of travel, resources, and expense and in no way refer to the value or legitimacy of a mission trip.)

Another question to consider is whether to travel to the inner city or a rural community? Each setting has different needs. (You aren't going to repair barns and silos in the inner city.) It's up to your group to determine to which location God is calling them.

Often a sudden need determines the project, as was the case with the Asian tsunami and Hurricane Katrina. Sometimes a need is so great that you don't have much choice in where to go; if you want to do hurricane cleanup in the United States, you'll head to the Southeast.

## MISSION: WHO?

God calls everyone and can use everyone. So do not under any circumstance set a religious or financial mark that has to be met to be worthy enough to participate. Ultimately none of us is worthy, "since all have sinned and fall short of the glory of God; they are now justified by [God's] grace as a gift, through the redemption that is in Christ Jesus" (**Romans 3:23-24**).

The dynamic of a mission trip changes according to which age groups participate. For example, a trip designed for adults and youth is going to be different from a trip designed for youth alone (with chaperones, of course). A trip for high school youth is going to be different from a trip for junior high or middle school youth. A family trip is going to be . . . OK, you get the idea. The best way for you to determine who should participate is to ask yourself, What does God want to do in our group through this experience? The answer to that question will give you the best idea about who should go on the trip.

Sometimes organizations will have a minimum age requirement, which would have an impact upon the eligibility of the participants. (See pages 109–111 for a list of groups that organize mission trips.) If your church or youth group is small, you may have only the option of a junior and senior high combined trip. Or, your group may be too large for a combined trip and you have to split the youth for two separate trips. The destination may influence whom you decide should go on the trip. Do you want to take junior high youth out of the country, only high school youth, or only juniors and seniors?

**READY-TO-GO MISSIONS**

# The Practical Basics of Planning a Mission

There are a two main ways to do a mission: plug-and-play and do-it-yourself. For a plug-and-play mission, you sign up through an organization that runs the project. When you arrive at the site, the agency plugs you into the system for a set amount of time. Typically, the sponsor organization takes care of work projects, food, lodging, and, sometimes, the spiritual programming for the trip. For a do-it-yourself mission, you and your group make all the arrangements and take care of all the details. You arrange lodging, cook your own meals, arrange work projects, and lead the spiritual programs. In this section, you'll learn tools to use for either type of mission.

## PLANNING

When planning a mission, involve your group. You can plan a whole trip and just put it out there in front of them, and you'll probably get some takers. But if you bring them in on the planning and let them have ownership of the trip, they will have more enthusiasm when it comes time to participate.

For even more participation, get pastoral and parental support for the trip early on. Again, you can put a mission idea out there; but if you have pastoral and parental support for the trip from the get-go, involvement and participation will be much greater. And having pastors and parents behind the project makes recruiting chaperones and fundraising easier.

To involve all of these people and make plans, you must start early. If you're looking to take a summer mission trip, start planning by at least October. Many groups start planning a year or more out. Build a timeline and schedule like the one on page 107. And as long as you're getting an early start, recruit volunteers and chaperones early too, especially since most adult volunteers will have to take vacation from work to go with you.

Once you start planning a trip, the two most common questions you'll hear are, "Where are we going?" and "How much does it cost?" Read on for some helpful guides in determining the answer to those questions.

## DESTINATIONS

There are three main categories of destinations: local, national, and international. Think about a few things before you pick a place. Is your group going to continue doing mission trips? If so, does your group want to go to the same place each year or do you want to change locations every year? Each option has its pros and cons. Youth returning to the same place for a third, fourth, or fifth year have a deep connection to the work site, the people, and the community. On the other hand, if you change locations and projects each year, the youth will experience something new, gaining a broader scope of the diverse needs and conditions in the world.

Both approaches to mission-trip destinations have value. If one doesn't seem to work well for your group, try the other. Remember to let youth have a say in the decision.

## COST

**Warning:** You are entering a sensitive area. The number-one reason youth don't go on a mission trip is . . . guesses? . . . Anyone? . . . Bueller? . . . Bueller? That's right—the cost.

So how do you handle this unavoidable part of a mission trip, when most youth don't have a steady stream of income?

Money should not and cannot be the reason for not participating. When you honor God, God honors you. If you're trying to do what God asks of you, then you have to have faith that God will provide the money to make it happen. Now that you're not going to let money be an excuse, how do you go about coming up with the money?

First, budget responsibly. This step doesn't mean finding the cheapest options; it means being good stewards of your resources. Take into account travel, lodging, fuel, program expenses, building materials, project costs, and so on. Use the Cost-Estimation Sample (page 96) as an example of how to determine the cost for a trip.

There will always be things that you didn't (or couldn't) account for. So always build a little extra into the budget for unexpected items that come up. Gas may be $3.00 a gallon now, but what will it cost when you're in the middle of nowhere with only one station? When estimating, budget for fifty cents a gallon more than current prices. It's better to have money left over for next year's trip than to run out of money on this year's trip.

Another factor affecting the cost of your trip is the number of participants. Consider how many chaperones and volunteers you'll need on the trip and whether adult leaders are responsible for paying their own way or the group is paying for part or all of the adults' fees. If you choose the latter option, include the cost for the adult participants in the overall trip budget.

If you are doing a plug-and-play mission trip, include the organization's registration fee in your cost estimation. This fee usually includes lodging at the event, meals at the event, building materials, and program needs. It does not include meals, lodging, and travel to and from the destination.

Youth groups often include a fun activity tacked on at the end of a mission trip. For example, a group coming back from Mexico may stop at an amusement park in southern California. Or a group in northern Arizona may swing by the Grand Canyon. If you are planning on a little extra activity just for fun, include it in the cost of the trip.

## TRAVEL

Since teleporters don't exist and Scotty can't beam your group to its location, you'll have to do things the old fashioned way. Travel can be the largest chunk of your costs if you have far to go; but you have lots of options, some more economical than others.

Air is usually the most expensive but quickest way to travel. Keep in mind your ground transportation needs when you arrive at your destination. Air travel also can limit the supplies you bring. Call the airline to see about checking those pickaxes and shovels before you arrive at the airport and meet Mr. and Mrs. TSA. Sometimes you have to fly because driving is not feasible. So if you are flying during your trip, check with the airlines or a travel agent about group tickets. Most airlines offer group tickets and rates for ten or more people.

Or your group might take a train. This option is a fun way to see the country, and most teens have never taken a long train ride. The downside to rail travel is that it takes longer than flying. But if you have the time, the train is a great, economical way to travel. Just be forewarned that trains frequently run late; make sure you don't have any short layovers, or you'll miss your connection.

Rail travel allows you more than just one checked bag and a carry on. It also gives your group time to spend together before and after the trip. The youth can enjoy dining cars, lounges, observation cars, sleeping cars, private rooms, and common areas where they can read, play games, watch movies, or just sit and watch God's beautiful world pass by one clickity-clack at a time.

Often the least expensive option for travel is by automobile. When you drive, you don't have to pay for multiple plane tickets and rental vehicles when you arrive. Your cost for travel is the same whether you're driving a van with one or ten passengers. Your gas mileage will be lower the heavier you load up; but for the most part, driving costs the same no matter how many people go.

Of course, the cost for driving depends on the number of vehicles, the number of miles, the terrain (mountain, flat land, interstate, or dirt roads), and the cost of fuel. With gas prices on the rise, driving may cost too much; check the numbers before making a final decision. (Know, for instance, that most twelve- to fifteen-passenger vans get ten to fifteen miles per gallon on the interstate.) And, on the downside, driving takes longer, requiring youth to be cooped up for long periods of time and tiring the drivers. But these times of close proximity can spur relationship building.

If you do drive, take advantage of the flexibility to change routes and visit any attractions along the way. If you're driving through South Dakota on your way to a mission site in Montana, swing by Mount Rushmore and let the kids see this beautiful tribute. Or if you're driving past LaCrosse, Kansas, visit the Barbed Wire Museum and Hall of Fame. Look for other fine attractions across the US, such as Wall Drug, The Corn Palace, Rock City, and The Thing.

## LODGING

Hotels are the most comfortable place to stay, but they're usually the most expensive. To keep the costs down, check with national chains and ask about group rates; or have your group double, triple, and quadruple up on room occupancy. Two double beds mean four people of the same sex can share the room. And don't forget the roll-away beds; sometimes you can put more than one of them in a room. If you have a large group, ask the hotel whether it has an unused conference room where your group can stay. If so, put the guys on one side, and the girls on the other. If the hotel offers two separate conference rooms, designate one for girls and one for guys.

If hotel lodging doesn't suit your budget, find churches along your route where you can stay the night, since most churches don't charge for their floor space. Finding a church is easy if you have Internet access. When contacting the church, find out whether they have showers or a kitchen facility that you can use, or find out whether a nearby community center has showers. Make contact well in advance, because most churches have a process for approving requests for sleeping space and it often takes a month to get an answer. If the church does not charge a fee, leave a donation ($25–$50), along with a thank you card. Build the donation or the church's fee into the cost of the trip.

Sometimes, churches will put youth into church members' homes. These families usually host one to four youth for the night. And many times those the families will feed them breakfast in the morning.

Other options for lodging include campgrounds, YMCA or YWCA, Kampgrounds of America, or homes of your church members' relatives. Find out whether any of the participants on the trip have relatives along the way. If they do, you have a great lead in finding a place to sleep.

## BEFORE AND AFTER

Most people think that a mission trip begins and ends on the actual dates of the trip. But to have the fullest experience possible, the work begins long before the trip and continues after the mission team returns home.

The months leading up to the mission and the months following can enrich your group's mission experience and can spur individual growth as well. So have proper preparation and discussion beforehand and a processing time following your trip.

# PREPARATION

In the time leading up to your mission, you'll have meetings for planning, including at least one for parents. At these times, you can discuss itinerary, costs, work projects, tool lists, contact information for emergencies, recommendations, travel arrangements, and so on. You can also communicate any precautions and immunization recommendations based on travel advisories from the Centers for Disease Control.

Use the time leading up to your trip to begin moving youth into deeper, closer relationships with one another, with the people they are going to serve, and with God. Here are some ideas:

→ Schedule individual and group prayer time where you can pray for the coming trip.

→ Lead a Bible study targeting the trip's principles and focuses.

→ Create devotions that the youth can do at home or together. Or better yet, have the youth create a devotion booklet to be used during the mission trip.

→ Ask each youth to prepare a one-page report on a different aspect of the coming trip, so that the group has a better understanding of the history and culture of the people you're serving. For instance, if you're headed to an Indian reservation, have the youth prepare reports to show the group.

→ Encourage the youth to keep a journal where they can write about their excitement, nervousness, fears, and hopes regarding the trip. They can also write prayers for their friends going along; the leaders of the mission; and those who will receive the love, service, and outreach.

→ Create a covenant among the participants. This covenant should include expectations for behavior, appropriate clothing, participation in scheduled activities, and curfew. It should also include consequences for those breaking the covenant, such as being sent home early. Involve as much of the group as possible when creating this agreement. Clearly communicate that adult leaders, chaperones, and volunteers must abide by the covenant too.

Start the bonding and growth process in the months leading up to your mission, and your youth will get even more out of their time together on the trip.

# GET THE WHOLE CHURCH INVOLVED

Even if only the youth and some parents are going on the trip, the entire church can be a part of the mission effort. Having the pastor's support will go a long way in making your trip the best it can be. Having the whole church behind you will make it even better. So find creative ways to involve the church.

If your group doesn't want to ask for money, have a collection drive for tools or supplies. If you need nail aprons, find out whether your church has a sewing group whose members would enjoy making aprons for the youth. Do you need a luggage rack on the church van? Maybe someone in the church is a welder. Do you need chaperones who aren't parents of youth? Look for adults of various ages and abilities. Be creative in your search; your congregation will be amazed at how it can contribute beyond money.

# FUNDRAISING

For some people, this part of missions causes the most anxiety. Most youth don't have a steady source of income allowing them to put lots of money away for things like mission trips. And if they do have money, they're usually saving for college and other important things—video games, clothes, MP3s, and so on. So you need a way for the teens to earn the money to go on the trip.

First, have the youth make a financial contribution, even if it's small. They need to decide whether to buy that new pair of shoes or put money toward a mission trip. When teens invest in a trip, they tend to have more enthusiasm about it. You can determine what amount or percentage the youth should pay; but keep in mind that some youth and their families may not be able to pay anything, so make alternative arrangements privately. And be sensitive to families with more than one youth participating in the trip.

On top of having the youth come up with some money, you can have them raise funds. Doing so will require them to tell others about what they're doing and why—evangelism at the simplest level. So find the balance that works best for your group. For a trip that costs $600 a person, you might make each youth responsible for $100 and have him or her participate in fundraisers to come up with the remaining $500.

So how do you go about mission-trip fundraising? Approach it from the perspective of team building. See the project as a way to bring your youth together for a sense of cohesion early on.

In addition to fundraising events, many churches offer scholarships through their missions team or endowment funds. See whether your church has such a fund for which the youth can apply. While you're at it, check out the many regional and national organizations that have scholarship monies available.

To involve the youth in the work, have them write letters to their extended family and friends. The messages should provide information about the mission trip and an invitation to make a tax-deductible donation to your trip through the church. Or perhaps a grant writer in your congregation could assist. Youth leaders often overlook grants, which require more work to obtain; but if the money's out there, hey, why not use it?

One last note on fundraising: Some youth groups credit money from specific fundraisers to the personal fee of only those who participated in that fundraiser. So if five youth help with yardwork for a total of $200, each youth receives $40 toward the mission-trip fee. Or you could give each teen credit according to how many hours he or she has worked. To come up with the wage, add up the total hours worked by the youth group; then divide the total profits by the number of hours to get a dollar-per-hour rate. To figure how much to credit each youth, multiply the wage by the number of hours he or she has worked. This credit method rewards those who work the fundraisers and prevents animosity between youth who do fundraising and those who don't but have their fee paid for.

## MEALS

During a mission trip, stopping at restaurants is easier but not necessarily cheaper. Fast food works great for lunch when you're on the road. But a trip to a local grocery store is usually a more nutritious and less expensive option for breakfast and dinner. Of course, cooking requires the right facilities.

If you don't have a dedicated kitchen team on site, divide the youth into teams and have each team make meals throughout the mission. Here is an example of a meal prep schedule:

> **Day 1:** Breakfast (Team 1), Lunch (Team 2), Dinner (Team 3)
>
> **Day 2:** Breakfast (Team 2), Lunch (Team 3), Dinner (Team 1)
>
> **Day 3:** Breakfast (Team 3), Lunch (Team 1), Dinner (Team 2)
>
> **Day 4:** Breakfast (Team 1), Lunch (Team 2), Dinner (Team 3)
>
> **Day 5:** Breakfast (Team 2), Lunch (Team 3), Dinner (Team 1)

Plan easy, healthful meals that teens like, and plan to use leftovers. (Salsa tastes good on potatoes as well as burritos.) If you're on site for lunch without refrigeration, plan accordingly. Nothing ruins a good day of repairing an outhouse more than spending the afternoon in the outhouse because of a bad egg salad sandwich.

## FOLLOW-UP

Follow-up after a trip is just as important as the preparation. Unfortunately, youth leaders are often so exhausted from the trip that when they get back, they consider the trip finished. But this point is when the important work begins. You have this awesome, life-changing, shared experience to build on—take advantage of it.

Before the trip, plan follow-up activities; as soon as you get back, implement them. If you try to create something after you get back, you'll be too tired and will keep putting it off with the best intentions of doing it tomorrow. Plus, your teens' excitement about the trip will diminish with each passing day. So plan ahead and be ready to strike while the iron's hot. You won't have all the details, because the trip hasn't happened yet; but if you have a general plan, you can easily plug in the specifics.

Plan a Bible study that focuses on what the youth have learned and discovered on the trip. Or create a devotion booklet that takes them back through the trip one day at a time. You can even revisit the devotions you did before the trip so that the youth can compare their pre- and post-trip views and feelings. If the youth took photos on the trip, have them create a poster or collage. These reflection times can help the youth individually process what they experienced and discover what the shared experience means for the future of the group.

Follow up with those who supported you and your mission experience financially, through volunteering time or services, through prayer, or in any other way. You might present a slide show to these folks. And be forewarned that a slide show nowadays does not involve actual slides but a computer (which begs the question, Why isn't it called a computer show?) Anyway, use this time to show photos or videos from the trip and to let the youth tell stories and give testimonies.

To let the whole church know about the mission, have the youth report on the trip during regularly scheduled worship services. The teens can talk for just a few minutes or preach the morning's message from the pulpit. Or have the youth write letters for the church newsletter and website, reporting what they did on the trip, what they learned, and how it has had an impact on their faith. If your group loves scrapbooking, have the youth prepare some scrapbooks of your mission; make them available for church members to look through, and ask the youth to be there to answer questions about the trip. As part of your follow-up with the youth, have them come up with ideas and plans for talking about their experience with supporters.

After the youth tell the church about the mission, continue the connection with the mission site. With the youth, brainstorm ways in which they, individuals, or members of the church can do so. If you worked at an orphanage, perhaps you can organize a clothing or supplies drive that benefits the charity. Such an ongoing mission involves more people than were able to go on the trip. And if you're returning to the same site each year, these projects will help the teens stay connected between trips.

## PASSING ON THE VISION

We talked about follow-up, but passing on the vision is what takes a mission trip full circle. Have the youth plan ways to get others involved in the ongoing connection to the mission site or to join future mission trips. These people might be youth and adults in your church as well as other churches. Encourage your teens to visit other youth groups and show them photos, videos, or a slide show, answering any questions the groups have.

And why not invite another youth group to go on the trip with you? Even if just one or two youth and an adult chaperone join you, they'll come back and get their group and church excited about doing a mission trip.

## NOTE ABOUT INTERNATIONAL TRAVEL

If you're going overseas, find out the current requirements for entering a foreign country and re-entering the United States, such as passports, visas (not always necessary) and notarized letters allowing minors to leave the US without their parents or legal guardians See the Sample Notary Form for International Travel With Minors (page 103).

Also, check with the CDC (1-800-CDC-INFO, or *www.cdc.gov*) for immunization recommendations for travel abroad.

# Ready to Go

## Short-Term Missions (1-3 Days)

# MAKE-A-DIFFERENCE DAY

*I can do all things through him who strengthens me.*
*(Philippians 4:13)*

**Project Description:** Help your youth learn the lesson of "a little goes a long way" by doing yardwork for people in your area who can't do it for themselves. If you live in a city of high rises, choose projects such as house cleaning, a clothing drive, and a food bank. You want your students to understand that seemingly small tasks can make a huge difference.

**Destination and Duration:** Your local community; a full day of work

**Travel and Cost:** Minimal, depending on the mission project's needs, such as supplies, food, and transportation

**Get the Whole Church Involved:** Seek the congregation's assistance in collecting tools or supplies ahead of time. If your group project involves collecting food or clothes, invite everyone to make donations. Enlist the help of church members to provide lunch for the youth. Pair up youth and older adults from your church, and have them pray for each other. Set up a prayer vigil where church members can sign up to pray during a specific time slot, so that someone is praying for the entire duration of the mission.

# PREPARATION

➜ Use at least one regularly scheduled youth group meeting to decide on a project. Ask youth with strong leadership skills to organize, recruit, and lead other youth in various aspects of the project. Ask church members to pray for the mission group and the recipients of the service provided.

➜ Have the teens memorize the key Scripture verse and pray for strength to do whatever it takes to make a difference.

➜ In the weeks leading up to Make-a-Difference Day, lead your group through a Bible Study that focuses on people who made a difference or on the ways Jesus did so in the lives of those he encountered.

➜ Some youth may not know how to use a lawn mover, garden spade, or leaf blower. Set up a time when the students can come together and learn how to properly, effectively, and safely operate the tools they will be using on the mission. Enlist the help of a professional gardener or landscape specialist to teach the necessary techniques. For fun, enlist the help of a groundskeeper from a local school, professional sports arena, or public parks department. Have them teach youth the "secret" to getting that "ballpark" look.

# SCHEDULE FOR THE DAY

**Gathering Time:** Before doing any work on the day of your mission, prepare your hearts for what God can do through your group. Read the key Scripture verse, and talk about the strength that we have in Christ to accomplish any task, no mater how great or small.

Spend time in prayer, asking for strength to go out and make a difference in someone's life and in the students' lives while they serve others.

**Work, Eat Lunch, Work Some More:** If you've divided into smaller groups to work in the same community, meet up for lunch at a fast-food place or bring lunch with you and meet at a park.

**End of the Day:** When the teens have finished working and put the tools away, discuss the highs and lows of the day and how the youth encountered God. If your students were divided into smaller groups and did multiple projects, begin by having each group report what it did on its worksite.

Here are some questions to guide your discussion:

➜ What was the best part of your day? What was the hardest or most challenging part of your day? Why?

➜ What in your day was something you didn't expect?

➜ Other than the main project itself, what did you do today that made an impression on someone else?

➜ Did you encounter someone who made an impression on you? If so, how did he or she do so?

➜ How did you make a spiritual impression today—or did you?

➜ How have you grown or changed in your faith because of what you did today?

➜ How can the little things you did today have an impact on your life and the lives of others in the future?

➜ Overall, do you feel like you've made a difference today? Why, or why not?

➜ How can you take what you've experienced today and use it to continue making a difference? Come up with at least one specific thing you can do to follow up on this day.

Remind your group that while it's nice to see the difference they've made right away, as with cleaning up a yard, sometimes we don't get to see the full impact of our actions for a long time. Your group's actions of love may inspire others to do the same down the road, so you've made a difference that lasts long after you're done with the project.

## FOLLOW-UP

Two weeks after your Make-a-Difference Day, check back with the participants to see how their experience has changed their approach to helping others. Ask the youth what little things they are doing to make a difference every day.

Another way to reinforce and refocus the youth on their mission experience is to have participants prepare a devotion to lead at youth group.

Or have each participant write a devotion with reflections on his or her learnings and growth in faith because of the mission. Compile these reflections into a devotion booklet, and distribute them to members of the youth group and the church.

Follow up with church members by giving a report at a worship service, in a newsletter article, through a special presentation to the church, or in all of these ways. Make sure youth include how they've been changed and how they are continuing to make a difference in the world.

Finish the report with an invitation to the whole church to join in on next year's Make-a-Difference Day.

# THE INFLUENCE OF AFFLUENCE

*Therefore, I urge you, in view of God's mercy, to offer your bodies as living sacrifices, holy and pleasing to God—this is your spiritual act of worship. Do not conform any longer to the pattern of this world, but be transformed by the renewing of your mind. Then you will be able to test and approve what God's will is—his good, pleasing and perfect will.*

*(Romans 12:1-2, NIV)*

**Project Description:** This project will help your youth consider these influences in their lives: friends, family, money, media, and Christ.

Partner with a church that needs basic repair, maintenance, painting, or yard clean-up but doesn't have the personal or financial resources to do the work. Be careful not to approach this project with a "we're going to help 'them' " attitude. You want your youth to have a servant's heart and see themselves as partners with the other church in ministry together.

**Destination and Duration:** A church in your community that could use some help for two to three days, such as a Friday to Sunday

**Travel and Cost:** Minimal, depending on the needs of the church you are serving, as well as meals and gasoline.

If you can, arrange to stay at the church where you are working or at a nearby church, shelter, or hotel. If your worksite is close to your church, stay at your own church and commute to the worksite each day.

**Get the Whole Church Involved:** Encourage your congregation to provide needs specific to the project. If you are doing grounds maintenance, have a plant or flower drive where church members can donate plants, trees, or bulbs to be planted at the mission site. If you are doing construction, ask people to donate money for covering a room with dry wall, for example.

As with any trip, coordinate church members to bring meals to youth on site. Or invite both congregations (your home church and the church at which you are working) to gather together for a barbeque or picnic celebrating the work that's been done.

# PREPARATION

➔ For one week prior to the trip, have the youth keep a journal of how they spend their money, including where they spent their money and what they bought. Also have them keep a record of how they spend their time, including what they watched on TV and how much time they spent on the computer (not counting homework).

As always, involve the teens in the development of the mission. Take them with you when you meet with the pastor of the local church to determine the projects. Have the students announce, recruit, and encourage other youth to participate.

➔ Make sure that all permission slips, medical release forms and any other forms are turned in and ready to go. Double check that all food and work supplies are ready to be used on the worksite.

➔ Invite your church members to pray for the mission team, the church being served, its members, and its witness in the world. With your group, pray for the people who will benefit from the improvements.

➔ Lead your group in Bible study examining the key Scriptures for the mission; ask your teens to think about the influences in their lives and how the youth might become influential in doing God's work.

➔ Some how-to classes in the weeks before the mission may help get a quicker start once you are onsite. Teach the mission team how to, for example, use paint rollers, hang dry wall, or prune trees.

➔ Train your team in how to show their faith to others, which can span from preaching to just offering a positive Christian example. Everyone will have a different level of comfort in this area—that's fine.

## SCHEDULE FOR THE TRIP

Day 1 (Friday Evening)

Gathering, traveling, arrival time

Session 1: rules, expectations, schedule

Organizing the supplies

Group-building activity or game

Snacks

Worship

Brush and flush

Lights out

## Day 2 (Saturday)

Rise, shine, breakfast

Session 2: The Influence of Friends and Family. (See the Discussion Questions, pages 31–32.)

Work, eat, work some more, eat some more

Session 3: The Influence of Money and the Media (See pages 32–33.)

Group-building activity or game

Snacks

Worship

Games or movies

Brush and flush

Lights out

## Day 3 (Sunday Morning)

Rise, shine, breakfast

Session 4: The Influence of Christ (See pages 33–34.)

Closing worship

Clean up and load up

Departure

## SESSION DISCUSSION QUESTIONS

### The Influence of Friends and Family

Help the youth think about the influences in their lives and how easily the youth are swayed in their decision making and how the influential people in their lives see and treat others.

Ask:

➔ Who is the most influential person in your life? Why?

➔ How do your family members influence you?

➜ How do your friends influence you?

➜ How are they the same? How are they different?

➜ Do you listen to one more than the other?

➜ When it comes to spiritual things, do you turn to your friends, or to your family? If neither, then whom do you turn to?

➜ If your friends aren't good influences, what can you do?

➜ If your family isn't being a good influence, what can you do?

➜ Why must we "not conform any longer to the pattern of this world, but be transformed" (Romans 12:2a, NIV)?

## The Influence of Money and Media

Begin this session by having an adult leader show the teens something that was a "must-have, hot thing" when he or she was a youth. The item might be a Cabbage Patch Kid or Teddy Ruxpin, an early VCR or Atari video-game system, or a pair of stone-washed jeans. The past appeal of the object should seem ridiculous and make the youth laugh. (If you can't find a once-hot item or don't want to spend too much money on eBay, just find a picture of it.)

As you pass the item around, tell everyone how cool it was and how you just had to have it. Mention how you saved money for a month or stood in line for hours just to get it.

Ask the youth about current trends and must-haves. If you had the teens write in their journal (described in the preparation section), use this time to discuss how they spent their time and money.

Ask:

➜ If you won a $1,000 shopping spree, at which store would you shop? Why? Be specific—"the mall" doesn't count.

➜ If you could have any car, what would you choose to drive?

➜ What is your favorite TV show?

Move deeper in your discussion with these questions:

➜ How does the media—TV, magazines, movies, the Web, and so on—influence our culture? How does it influence you personally?

➜ If it doesn't influence you, how do you determine what clothing style is "in"? what music is popular? which cell phone is hot?

➜ How do money and media influence your faith?

➜ How does your faith influence your approach to money and media?

➜ John Wesley, one of the Reformers, said that we should earn all we can, save all we can, and give all we can. How does that saying compare to our culture's approach to money?

➜ Does the media affect how you treat people? What about the "dominant ideology" that exists in our society? It says that some people are better than others—for example, that the rich are are superior to the poor, white to non-white, male to female, straight to gay, and skinny to overweight.

➜ How can you let God rather than media influence how you view others? What would your youth group look like if God's standards were used instead of the media's?

## The Influence of Christ
Too often everything but Christ influences our daily lives. In fact, sometimes the only time we remember God is on Sunday mornings—and even then, sometimes we're so mad at our parents for "forcing" us to go to church that we still don't seek God's influence.

Use these questions to help your group realize that God wants to be our companion and empower us to "do justice, and to love kindness, and to walk humbly with ... God" (**Micah 6:8b**).

➜ Where does Christ fit when it comes to influences in your life?

➜ If we know that God should be the primary influence in our lives, why do we resist letting God be number one?

➜ What areas of your life are the easiest for you to let Christ influence? Why?

→ What areas of your life are the hardest for you to let Christ influence? Why?

→ How can you change that problem and let Christ influence those areas?

→ How can you know what God wants? What role does prayer, Bible study, worship, and youth group play in helping you discover what God wants?

→ What are two specific things you are going to do to let Christ be your primary influence?

→ How might you live out doing justice, loving kindness, and walking humbly with your God?

Instead of or in addition to discussing the last two questions out loud, you may want to have the youth write down their answers. If so, give each of the students a writing utensil and a piece of paper.

After they are done writing, give them stamped envelopes; tell the youth to put their paper in an envelope, seal it, and address it to themselves. Then collect the envelopes and mail them to the youth at a later time. They will remember the mission-trip session once they're "back in the real world."

## FOLLOW-UP

Challenge the youth to give up TV or the Internet for a week or month. Then ask them what they did with their time. Did they miss TV, or not? Why? Ask them how their view of the world was changed and how their sacrifice had an impact on their faith. Relay the individual answers to the entire youth group and to the whole church.

As a group, give up shopping for one day, week, or month and collect the money youth were going to spend on themselves to be donated to the mission site or another worthy cause providing a service to others.

Invite your church members to visit the mission site and see the plants they provided once they're in place. Arrange a tour of rooms that were worked on so that the members can see in person what they helped to create. If a tour is not possible, create a large poster with plenty of before-and-after photos to show the supporters. If you challenge the mission participants to give up shopping and donate money they would have spent on themselves, encourage the entire church to join in or match the teens' level of sacrifice and giving.

# GIFT-A-PALOOZA

*Like good stewards of the manifold grace of God, serve one another with whatever gift each of you has received. . . . Whoever serves must do so with the strength that God supplies, so that God may be glorified in all things through Jesus Christ.*

*(1 Peter 4:10-11a)*

**Project Description:** Your youth are full of gifts that God has instilled in them. To help them use their gifts to serve others, have a multigenerational outreach celebration in your community. Host a weekend of workshops, art shows, cooking demonstrations, skateboard exhibitions, concerts, or whatever highlights the youths' talents.

**Destination and Duration:** Your home church and local neighborhood; one to two days

**Travel and Cost:** No travel; cost varies depending on the offerings you choose.

**Get the Whole Church Involved:**

➡ Invite the entire church. Make the event one big party where everyone can celebrate the gifts he or she has received from God.

➡ Recruit church members to lead workshops and share their wisdom. Perhaps someone in the congregation has been composing poems for years and would be perfect for a poetry writing workshop. Do any folks have talent in the kitchen? Have them lead a workshop on cooking or baking. Better yet, have them organize a feast of celebration that follows the display of gifts, with the class participants helping out.

➡ Enlist the prayers of the congregation for members of the mission team and the people they'll be working with. Pray for your church and its outreach to the community. Pray for the participants and the development of their gifts.

## PREPARATION

Help your teens discover, develop, and celebrate their gifts before taking on this project. Then they'll understand what to do for the festival's participants.

Lead the youth through a Bible study of **1 Corinthians 12:4-11.** Explore the difference between talents and spiritual gifts, perhaps leading the youth through a spiritual-gift assessment. Talk about how people can use talents, which are gifts from God, for the Lord. This discussion will guide your group in deciding what you will offer at the gift-a-palooza.

If you have some star musicians in your group, invite them to offer music; talented actors, a musical or play; athletes, a sports clinic. Other ideas for short courses include dance, organizing, and writing.

Once you decide on the workshops and venues, secure any supplies (such as instruments, sets, stands, ramps, and easels) that you'll need for the event. Your group may have to purchase some things, borrow others, or build them from scratch. For example, if some youth are doing skateboarding, you may have to build ramps, rails, or a half-pipe. If you're offering painting, you'll need brushes, canvas or paper, and easels. For singing and acting, you'll need a stage and sound equipment.

Publicize your gift-a-palooza, and take registrations in advance. Create a brochure highlighting the workshops, clinics, and exhibits being offered and explaining what the cost includes, if there is one.

Recruit adult volunteers to help with the workshops. Approach a local arts-and-crafts store, and see whether it will co-sponsor part of the event by providing supplies or special coupons for the participants.

With this mission, the youth will not only help others celebrate their gifts but will also have their own moments of discovery and growth, including when they prepare for the event.

## SAMPLE SCHEDULE

### Day 1

8:00 A.M.        Set up

9:00 A.M.        Registration, sign in, welcome

9:30 A.M.        Participants' rally (See Discovering Your Gifts, page 39.)
                 **Note:** At each participants' rally, briefly introduce the focus
                 (Discovering, Developing, Using, or Celebrating). Don't
                 make it too long or involved; just plant the seed of the idea.

10:00 A.M.       Workshop 1

| 12:00 P.M. | Lunch |
| 12:45 P.M. | Participants' rally (See Developing Your Gifts, page 39.) |
| 1:00 P.M. | Workshop 2 |
| 3:00 P.M. | Closing Rally |
| 3:30 P.M. | Participants leave |
| 3:30 P.M. | Clean up, replenish supplies, prepare for Day 2 |
| 4:30 P.M. | Mission-Team Small-Group Questions (See page 38.) |
| 5:30 P.M. | Close, and go home |

## Day 2

| 8:00 A.M. | Set up |
| 9:00 A.M. | Sign in, welcome |
| 9:30 A.M. | Participants' rally (See Using Your Gifts, page 39–40.) |
| 10:00 A.M. | Workshop 3 |
| 12:00 P.M. | Lunch |
| 12:45 P.M. | Participants' rally (See Celebrating Your Gifts, page 40.) Focus on the idea that gifts should be shared with others, not held in and limited. You may want to have a small token or other gift to present to each participant as a reminder of his or her gifts and experience on this mission. |
| 1:30 P.M. | Workshop 4 |
| 4:00 P.M. | Gather for snacks; organize for gift show |
| 4:30 P.M. | Gift show (where the participants showcase what they've learned, like in a talent show) |
| 6:00 P.M. | Feast for everyone |
| 7:00 P.M. | Participants leave |
| 7:00 P.M. | Clean up |
| 8:30 P.M. | Mission-Team Small-Group Questions (See page 38–39.) |
| 9:00 P.M. | Close, and go home |

## MISSION-TEAM SMALL-GROUP QUESTIONS, DAY 1

➡ What went well today? What did you struggle with?

➡ How were the workshops? Do you need to do anything differently tomorrow?

➡ What gifts did you discover in the participants?

➡ What gifts did you discover that you didn't expect?

➡ Do you feel that you are helping the participants develop their gifts? Why, or why not?

➡ How does God help us point out the gifts in others?

➡ What are your hopes for tomorrow? Do you have any apprehensions?

➡ What prayers do you want or need for tomorrow?

Close in group prayer (or in prayer partners), lifting up the concerns, hopes, and fears mentioned. Pray for the participants and their families.

## MISSION-TEAM SMALL-GROUP QUESTIONS, DAY 2

➡ How was your day? Did things go well?

➡ How did God use you and your gifts today?

➡ How did you facilitate others in using their gifts? Did you use God as a resource? Why, or why not?

➡ How did the gift show go? Was it a good celebration of our gifts?

➡ What gift did you use most during this mission?

➡ After this mission, what is one gift you discovered you want to develop more?

→ What have you learned about our different gifts all contributing to the big picture? How do they all fit together?

→ How are you going to continue using your gifts for others?

Close in prayer as a group.

# DISCUSSION QUESTIONS

**Discovering Your Gifts**

→ If you could have one super power, what would you choose? Why?

→ What gifts do you have?

→ What gifts do you wish you had?

→ How did you discover you were good at something?

→ What role does God play in the gifts you have?

**Developing Your Gifts**

→ What is your least favorite subject in school? Why?

→ Are gifts just natural ability? Explain your answer.

→ How do you get better at things you're not good at?

→ Have you tried practicing what you're good at? If not, why not? If so, how did it go?

→ How can God help you develop your gifts? How can you invite God to help you do so?

**Using Your Gifts**

→ Would you describe yourself as loving the spotlight, or blending in with the crowd? Why?

→ Do others know of your gifts? Why, or why not?

→ How do you generally use your gifts? For personal enjoyment? For the benefit of others? For both? Explain.

→ How do you think God wants you to use your gifts?

→ What do you need to do to let God use your gifts more?

**Celebrating Your Gifts**

→ What are some things we commonly celebrate?

→ How is celebrating different from bragging?

→ Without having a big party, how can we celebrate our gifts?

→ How can you show your thankfulness to God for the gifts you've received?

→ How are you going to use your gifts as something you give to others rather than something you keep for yourself?

## FOLLOW-UP

Set aside room on a bulletin board at church to have mission-team members write about the various gifts they used on the mission and how the teens are continuing to use those gifts for others.

→ Have the youth trace their hands then write on those handprints the gifts they have received and are thankful for. Affix the handprints to a poster, and hang it in a place where lots of people can easily see it. At regular youth group meetings, choose someone to tell the group about what he or she wrote on a hand on the poster.

→ Invite the participants to show pictures and tell stories from Gift-a-Palooza in worship. Or ask some of these people to exhibit their gifts in worship. If you had a cooking workshop, let someone with a knack for cooking make bread to use for Communion one week. Let an artist paint or draw something and highlight it in worship. Have one of the workshop groups from Gift-a-Palooza come and display their gift in worship; you might highlight a different group once a month.

# REALITY BITES

*"There was a rich man who was dressed in purple and fine linen and lived in luxury every day. At his gate was laid a beggar named Lazarus, covered with sores and longing to eat what fell from the rich man's table. Even the dogs came and licked his sores.*

*"The time came when the beggar died and the angels carried him to Abraham's side. The rich man also died and was buried."*
*(Luke 16:19-22, NIV)*

**Project Description:** Help your youth understand hunger as a faith issue by hosting World Vision's 30 Hour Famine. You could also participate in the Crop Walk (*churchworldservice.org/CROP/index.html*), a potato drop, The Souper Bowl of Caring (*souperbowl.org*). Or your group could simply work at a food kitchen.

**Destination and Duration:** Your home church or local retreat center; thirty consecutive hours. 30 Hour Famine has a couple of official dates, but it can be done anytime during the year. Check out World Vision's website at *worldvision.org* or *30hourfamine.org*.

**Travel, Lodging, and Cost:** The only expenses associated with this mission are the gas for any travel, program supplies, and food for the meal at which you break the fast.

Arrange travel to a grocery store and to a local food bank. All other travel can be done walking. If you are staying offsite, you'll need to arrange travel to and from your mission site. Whether you are staying at your church or at a retreat center, make the appropriate arrangements.

**Get the Whole Church Involved:** Invite members of the congregation to fast at home during the same period of time as your 30 Hour Famine mission.

If you are doing a canned food drive, encourage the church members to contribute. If you need drivers, have church members shuttle the mission participants to the store and food bank.

Instead of having a pizza party to wrap up your experience, ask members of the congregation to prepare a home-cooked meal. Or have an all-church dinner, where the youth can talk about what they've experienced and learned over the thirty hours.

## PREPARATION

Visit *30hourfamine.org* to get all of the promotional and program materials.

If the youth (or parents) are worried about the length of time without food, have them talk to their family doctor. Or invite a doctor, nutrition specialist, or someone familiar with fasting to speak at a youth group meeting prior to the mission and to talk about fasting as a spiritual discipline. Most people can go thirty hours without food and not have any major medical problem. But for some people, that type of fast is impossible. If someone needs to eat, have some food available. If someone in your group needs extra attention during the thirty hours, invite one of his or her parents or a nurse to help chaperone.

Reassure the youth that thirty hours isn't really that long. The hardest part is getting past the hunger cravings the first few hours. If the teens can make it past that point, they can fast for the rest of the time. Plus, by following the sample schedule, you spend several hours asleep, and when you wake up you'll already have twenty-one hours down and only nine left.

Have plenty of water and 100% fruit juice on hand for the youth to keep their sugars and energy up. Have someone with experience at fasting provide guidelines and suggestions for safety during the thirty-hour famine.

## SAMPLE SCHEDULE

The program 30 Hour Famine recommends beginning at noon and ending the following day at 6:00 P.M.

**Friday**

| | |
|---|---|
| 12:00 P.M. | Begin fasting at school |
| 6:00 P.M. | Gather at the church |
| 6:30 P.M. | Check in and see how it's going so far |
| 7:00 P.M. | Group building (using a game that your group loves to play) |
| 7:30 P.M. | Hunger Awareness Activity (See pages 43–44.) |
| 8:15 P.M. | Bible study and prayer |
| 9:00 P.M. | Movie |
| 11:00 P.M. | Brush and flush |
| 11:30 P.M. | Lights out |

**Saturday**

| | |
|---|---|
| 9:30 A.M. | Rise and shine |
| 10:00 A.M. | Grocery List (See page 44.) |
| 10:30 A.M. | Food Scavenger Hunt (See page 44.) |
| 11:30 A.M. | Sort and prepare the items collected to be donated |
| 12:00 P.M. | Grocery Price Shopping (See pages 44–45.) |
| 1:00 P.M. | Return to church, and total up the lists. |
| 2:00 P.M. | Volunteer at a Food Bank (See page 45.) |
| 4:00 P.M. | Return to church |
| 4:30 P.M. | Discussion and Bible Study (See page 45.) |
| 5:30 P.M. | Clean up |
| 6:00 P.M. | Pizza celebration |

# ACTIVITIES

## Hunger Awareness

When you do the 30 Hour Famine through World Vision, the organization provides all the programming and resources you need for promoting, leading, and following up with the event. If you want to do your own programming, check out *worldvision.org* and *bread.org* (Bread for the World) for statistics, information, and ways to help reduce hunger and need in the world.

Begin an opening discussion by asking whether anyone has ever said, "Oh, man, I'm starving!" Let the youth answer; then move on to these questions:

➜ What does it mean to be hungry vs. starving vs. "I haven't had a Snickers bar in two hours"?

Read the statistics on world, national, and local hunger that you've researched. Ask the youth what they think of those numbers. Are they lower, or higher than they expected?

➜ Where have you seen hungry people? Have you seen any in our town?

➜ Why are there hungry people in the world?

After the youth have answered, share any information you've discovered about the amount of food wasted and why people go hungry.

Read **Luke 16:19-22** and other Scriptures to see what God has to say about hunger, the hungry, and our responsibility as Christians.

Ask,

→ What does God call us to do about hunger?

### Grocery List

Distribute copies of the Grocery List (page 102). Have the youth fill out the left side of each column, recreating a typical weekly grocery list for their family. Ask them to leave off the prices for now.

The youth should include food primarily, but they can include other items such as toiletries and other household supplies. Ask the youth to be specific; if they get a certain brand of peanut butter, have them write that brand down, not just "peanut butter." Most families shop once a week, but some shop more or less frequently; for an average, ask the youth to compose a list for one week.

### Food Scavenger Hunt

If you have a large group, divide it into smaller teams. Have the teams go into the local neighborhood and collect food items in the time allotted. Donate all items to a local food bank or shelter.

Declare everyone a winner for his or her effort to get food for hungry people.

### Grocery Price Shopping

Now take the youth to a grocery store. Choose one that several families in your church frequent. Have the students bring their lists, and give them one hour to find prices for each item on their list. Have the youth write the prices on the right side of their paper then meet back at a central location when they are done.

Head back to the church, and ask the students:

→ What surprised you when you were at the grocery store finding prices?

→ What didn't surprise you?

Next, ask the youth add up the prices on their list to discover how much each family typically spends on groceries in a week. Then ask them to multiply that number by four to find out how much they spend a month. Now, have the students multiply that product by twelve to see how much their families spend a year on groceries.

Now ask:

➡ How much of your list is necessity, and how much is "extras"?

➡ What on your list could you and your family do without?

## Volunteer at a Food Bank

Take your group to a local food bank, and volunteer for a couple hours. Most food banks have collections, sorting, and prep work that needs to be done during the week between days when they serve food, especially at larger food bank distribution centers. Find the right opportunity for your group.

## Discussion and Bible Study

After returning from volunteering, remind the youth that the purpose of this thirty-hour mission isn't to make them feel guilty about their lives but to help them realize the extent of the need and the breadth of the divide between the haves and have-nots.

Read **Luke 16:19-22**, and ask:

➡ What does God call us to do about hunger and need in the world?

➡ How are followers of Christ responsible for feeding the world's hungry?

➡ Be honest: How often do you consider how many people go hungry every day?

➡ What, if anything, are you going to do differently now?

➡ What is one step you and your family can take to help end hunger in the world?

Close in prayer, asking for strength to follow through on the steps the youth are going to take in fighting hunger. Celebrate a successful thirty hours with a pizza party or some other breaking of your fast.

## FOLLOW-UP

Encourage the youth and their families to set up a regular scheduled time for volunteering at a food bank, soup kitchen, or shelter. Have the youth sit down with their families and talk about ways they can make a difference in the world together. Maybe they'll decide to cut back on an "extra" on their grocery list and send the money to an organization that serves the hungry. Their effort might be a one-time thing, an every-other-month thing, a commitment for one year, or a permanent thing.

To give the the youth and families an idea of how much they throw away, invite them to scrape their plates, for one week, into a small container instead of the trash or garbage disposal. At the end of the week, have them weigh the container. This image will remind them of how much they waste. Remind the families that this activity is not intended to make them feel guilty but to remind them that we have to be aware of our excess and work to overcome hunger.

Try hosting a World Dinner. Look for the instructions in *Marking Milestones and Making Memories for Youth: Looking Back, Looking Forward* (Abingdon Press, 2004; ISBN 0-687-73992-6).

# BEING HOMELESS SOCKS

*Jesus . . . got up from the meal, took off his outer clothing, and wrapped a towel around his waist. After that, he poured water in a basin and began to wash his disciples' feet, drying them with the towel that was wrapped around him.*

*He came to Simon Peter, who said to him, "Lord, are you going to wash my feet?"*

*Jesus replied, "You do not realize now what I am doing, but later you will understand."*

*When he had finished washing their feet, he put on his clothes and returned to his place. "Do you understand what I have done for you?" he asked them. "You call me 'Teacher' and 'Lord,' and rightly so, for that is what I am. Now that I, your Lord and Teacher, have washed your feet, you also should wash one another's feet. I have set you an example that you should do as I have done for you."*

*(John 13:3-15, NIV)*

**Project Description:** This mission will help your youth see homelessness as a faith issue and will challenge them to follow Jesus' example of servanthood. You will have a sock drive then deliver the new socks to homeless persons. You may also want to serve dinner or lead worship at a local homeless shelter.

**Destination and Duration:** Local area with a homeless population; one to two days (or longer if your youth will want to continue this mission)

**Travel, Cost, and Lodging:** You'll have expenses associated with sock collection boxes and signs, food, and travel. Stay outside your local church in a roped-off area. (See Homeless Experience, pages 50–51, for more details.)

**Get the Whole Church Involved:** Encourage the congregation to donate socks to the cause. Have a special collection on Sunday morning during worship, and pray for those who will receive the socks.

If you can, coordinate the sock delivery with Valentine's Day and have the church make valentines to be given out with each pair of socks. You might form a team to start a clothes closet, where new and gently used clothing items are collected, cleaned, and given to homeless persons.

# PREPARATION

Have the youth find a local organization that serves the homeless in your community, and arrange a sock drive to aid that organization. If your community doesn't have such an organization, simply collect the socks and distribute them yourself.

Recruit locations around town to host collection boxes for two weeks leading up to your mission date. Put signs on the collection boxes to inform people of the collection, what it's for, who's doing it, who benefits from it, and the dates of collection. During your mission collect all the boxes and take the socks to the agency that works with homeless persons, or distribute them yourself.

Read the Homeless Experience (pages 50–51), decide how you will set up your version of the experience, and prepare accordingly.

# SAMPLE SCHEDULE

**Day 1**

| | |
|---|---|
| 6:00 P.M. | Homeless Experience Opening (page 50) |
| 6:30 P.M. | Small Group 1 Questions (page 52) |
| 7:30 P.M. | Guest speaker |
| 9:00 P.M. | Small Group 2 Questions (page 52) |
| 10:00 P.M. | Enter Homeless Experience (pages 50–51) |

**Day 2**

| | |
|---|---|
| 8:00 A.M. | Back inside for breakfast |
| 9:00 A.M. | Cleanup (page 51) |
| 10:00 A.M. | Small Group 3 Questions (page 52–53) |
| 11:00 A.M. | Collection-bin pickup |
| 12:30 P.M. | Lunch |
| 1:00 P.M. | Sort and count the socks |

1:30 P.M.        Sock delivery

3:00 P.M.        Small Group 4 Questions (page 53)

4:00 P.M.        Closing

5:00 P.M.        Go Home

# HOMELESS EXPERIENCE

## Opening

Begin the homeless experience by collecting shoes, coats, wallets, purses, and all personal items the youth may have brought with them (they should keep their socks). Lock up all the items in a safe place, and tell the youth that they'll get them back later. Next, give each youth two used plastic grocery-store bags for their feet. The bags can have holes, since rarely do homeless people have brand new bags to keep their feet dry. When you give the youth their bags, tell them that they can use them in any way they want but that those bags are the only two they get—all night.

**Note:** Some students will need access to their asthma inhalers or other medications, and some girls will need hygiene products overnight. Have a plan for allowing them to discreetly access what they need.

Divide the youth into small groups, and discuss the small-group questions (pages 52–53).

**Guest Speaker Option:** Invite a former homeless person or someone who works with homeless people to speak to the group. The guest should talk about living on the street, mentioning where they sleep, get food, go to the bathroom, and take showers, as well as health problems they commonly face. He or she should also speak about the way homeless persons are treated by others, misconceptions, stereotypes, and the truth about who is homeless. Wrap up this time with a question-and-answer session.

## Enter Homeless Experience

Now's the time when youth really get to experience homelessness. Bring out some old blankets, a few towels, a couple of jackets, two beaten and broken umbrellas, an odd number of mismatched old shoes, and some newspapers. Make sure there isn't enough for everyone to get one of each.

Throw all of the items into a pile on the floor, and tell youth that they can pick out stuff to help them "survive" the night. They will undoubtedly argue and fight over things; some youth will have several items and others will end up with nothing. Now take the students outside to a roped-off area set up to be their "streets" where they'll be "homeless" for the rest of the night.

This area should be roped off and free of car traffic. It should have enough cardboard boxes for everyone to sleep on or inside. Place all of the boxes in a garbage or recycling bin somewhere in the roped off area. Have one steel garbage can where a fire can be lit to help provide warmth, and provide plenty of firewood for the night. An adult must be stationed at the fire at all times, with a fire extinguisher and wet blankets within arms' reach.

By now the youth will be hungry, so let the youth know that food is available but that they have to scrounge for it. Make sure to place some food around the area in garbage cans (sanitized beforehand), on the ground, and in other unusual places. All the food should be safe to eat at room temperature, so that the teens don't get sick. A bucket of chicken or pieces of pizza from the refrigerator, placed outside at the last minute, would work.

Fill water bottles half way with clean water, but mix brown food coloring to make the water look dirty; then retighten the tops and serve by placing them around the area.

Don't tell the youth that the food is from the fridge or that the water is completely safe. They won't believe that you would serve them ground water and chicken from a dumpster.

Have plenty of parents work shifts to supervise and protect the youth throughout the night.


## Cleanup
Tidy up the area used for the Homeless Experience. Give back all the belongings you took from the youth, and let them have time to change and freshen up.


## Closing
You'll need tongue depressors (or popsicle sticks), markers, and glue. Instruct each person to write on the tongue depressor one thing he or she is going to do to help the homeless or to prevent homelessness. Then have the group work together to build a home with the depressors and glue, placing the depressors with the writing facing out. Make sure that everyone has a hand in building.

When the home is completed, have the youth find their piece of the house and, one at a time, tell the group the one thing they are going to do. Read the key Scripture passage, and talk about what being servant-leaders means—even when the task isn't pretty. Close in prayer, asking God to fill you with servant hearts.

### Small Group 1 Questions

➜ When I say, "homeless person," what's the first thing that comes to mind?

➜ Do you ever give money to a person holding a cardboard sign at a corner or at a stoplight? Why, or why not?

➜ When was the first time you can remember seeing a person who you knew was homeless?

➜ Describe the "average" homeless person. Who is it?

➜ Do you know someone who is now, or has ever, been homeless? If so, does he or she fit the descriptions we just mentioned?

### Small Group 2 Questions

➜ What did you think about the guest speaker? What were you surprised to hear? What didn't come as a shock?

➜ Does a homeless problem exist in America? in our community? If so, what's the problem? If not, why not?

➜ What might help solve the problem?

### Small Group 3 Questions

➜ What did you think about the Homeless Experience last night? What items did you end up with? How was the cardboard bed?

➜ What was the hardest thing about it? What was easier than you thought?

➜ Do you think you could handle being homeless for a week? a month? a year? Why, or why not?

➜ How has your view of homelessness changed because of your experience last night? If it hasn't changed, why not?

➜ How did your faith help you make it through the night? If you didn't lean on your faith in God, why didn't you?

➜ Do you think homeless people find having a faith difficult? Why, or why not?

➜ What kind of an impact do you think becoming homeless would have on your faith?

➜ How should followers of Christ deal with homelessness?

### Small Group 4 Questions

➜ How did you feel when delivering socks, knowing that they would help so many people?

➜ Did you ever think that socks could make such a difference?

➜ Other than clean, dry socks and a roof over their head, what else do homeless people need? (Move beyond the "get a job" answers to things such as laundry facilities, friends who care, a telephone, transportation, healthcare, medicine, counseling, and someone to trust in them.)

➜ What are we as Christians called to do, regarding the homeless?

➜ What can you as an individual do to help those who are homeless? What can your family, youth group, and church do?

➜ What can we do to prevent homelessness?

## FOLLOW-UP

Keep the home you built during the closing visible in the youth room as a reminder that some people don't have a home. Provide the youth (and church members) with a list of municipal, state, and national legislators to be contacted regarding the homeless situation in your town, state, and nation.

Ask your local school district whether your group can assist homeless students through an existing program. If one does not exist, start one. Find out the best way for your youth group and church to help homeless students in your area.

# TRAIL MIX

*"Enter through the narrow gate; for the gate is wide and the road is easy that leads to destruction, and there are many who take it. For the gate is narrow and the road is hard that leads to life, and there are few who find it."*

*(Matthew 7:13-14)*

**Project Description:** Help your youth look to God and follow "the road that leads to life." This trail-maintenance-and-restoration mission will bring to life the idea of walking that path.

**Destination and Duration:** An outdoor wilderness area; one to three days, preferably on Earth Day (April 22) or on Arbor Day (a date that varies year to year)

**Travel, Cost, and Lodging:** The cost depends on your project. Since the work of clearing a trail doesn't require extravagant program expenses, the biggest expenses should be travel and food.

Regarding travel, this mission requires only a drive to and from your location and a hike to and from the trailhead to the worksite. And if you're cleaning up a local park, school, or mile of highway, you won't have far to drive.

The schedule and length of your mission will depend on the project you choose and the proximity to your location. If you have to drive two to three hours to get to a trail or stream, you may not want to drive back that same day and limit the work time. But if you're cleaning up a local city park, one day might be the perfect length for your mission.

For a mission longer than a day, arrange to spend the night near the worksite or to camp out in tents.

**Get the Whole Church Involved:** Recruit volunteers to join the youth group in this mission. Your church probably has avid hikers or outdoor types. These people are perfect for this mission, because they already appreciate and cherish the outdoors. If you are doing a longer mission that involves camping out, enlist the help and resources of those who love to camp.

# PREPARATION

Contact an outdoor organization that has regular trail-repair projects. For example, try:

→ The Sierra Club *(sierraclub.org)*
→ The National Arbor Day Foundation® *(arborday.org)*
→ The Earth Day Network *(earthday.net)*
→ REI® *(rei.com)* or your local REI store
→ The USDA Forest Service *(fs.fed.us)*

After picking a site, arrange a day when the youth can learn how to use the tools needed for the project. You should also have someone with experience show the teens methods and techniques for successfully and safely accomplishing tasks on the mission (such as how to team lift that fallen tree so that nobody ends up trapped beneath the 900-pound tree trunk).

Have a tool drive to gather shovels, hoes, saws, and so on.

Have an expert in environment ministries talk to the group about the benefits of trail clearing and stream restoration to the ecosystem and humans.

Have the students prepare devotions based on times when they've gotten back on the narrow path that leads to God.

Invite your church to pray for the group as the youth examine the path they are on. Ask the congregation to pray that their eyes would be open, their hearts would hear God's message, and that youth would make the changes needed to walk with Christ on that narrow path.

In the months leading up to your mission, have a Bible study focused on decision making. Hone in on the importance of making wise choices, as well as their consequences (such as the impact on others).

To delve further, point out the people in the Bible who made poor choices along the path of their lives. The best part of this study is that it's the story of all of us. We all do things we shouldn't; but despite our wandering from the narrow path, God still lets us get back on the path that leads to everlasting life. You cannot stress that point enough!

## SAMPLE SCHEDULE

Gather and load up

Depart for mission site

Onsite work

Lunch

Devotion and discussion questions (below)

Onsite work

Load up and return to church

Closing (next page)


## DISCUSSION AND DISCUSSION

An outdoor setting will make this part of your mission more powerful. Begin your discussion by having a youth share a devotion that he or she has prepared ahead of time that focuses on the main Scripture for the mission.

Then move the group through the following questions:

➔ Where's one of your favorite places to vacation? Why? If you don't have a favorite place, where would you choose to go if you could vacation anywhere in the world? Why?

➔ Have you ever gotten lost? Where, when, and what did you do?

➔ Have you ever gotten lost spiritually? How is it similar to being lost physically, like in an unfamiliar neighborhood?

➔ If God has a path for us but we're lost, how can we find that path and follow it? How can we "ask someone for directions" in this situation?

➔ How is the Bible a map for us?

➔ How else can you find your way and know that you are following the narrow road that God wants? How can you tell if you are on the broad path that leads to destruction?

→ How is it going on the worksite? What challenges have you faced so far? What seems to be working well?

→ Do you feel like you're making a difference? Why, or why not?

→ What other observations do you have about your work so far? What have you noticed about the trail?

## CLOSING

→ How did it go at your worksite this afternoon? What was the trail like before and after your work?

→ What was one of the hardest challenges you faced while clearing the path? How did you overcome it—or did you?

→ To overcome obstacles, you have to know what to do when you encounter one. Where can you find out how to handle the stumbling blocks that come into your life?

→ If the Bible is like a trail map, what or who are the trail markers and signposts that provide direction and guidance for you? Do you turn to the same people each time you need spiritual direction? Why, or why not?

→ Do you ever ask God for guidance and direction? Why, or why not? What was the result?

→ If you were a signpost, would you point others toward the narrow path, or the wide path? Why?

→ How have others made it easier for you to find and stay on the narrow path? Why are they important?

→ Why is surrounding yourself with Christian friends and family important?

→ How has (or will) your work today help others follow the trail and not get lost?

→ What obstacles in your life need clearing so that you can help others see and follow the path that leads to God?

## FOLLOW-UP

Set up accountability groups for those who go on the mission trip, so that they may keep one another on the narrow path. Provide a regular meeting time, such as once a month, for the accountability groups to gather and check in with one another. Once these groups are up and going, open them up for other youth from your group to join.

To let the rest of the church know about the mission, start a signpost project. Have the students take photos of people who help them to stay headed in the right direction. Attach the photos to a bulletin board designed with a signpost.

Or build a wooden signpost and attach the photos to all sides of it. Place the display in the sanctuary or at the entrance to your church. Tell the congregation about the signpost project, and invite the members to look at the photos and signpost as they pass by.

Have the youth present stories of how their supporters have helped them find or stay on the narrow path. Celebrate the congregation and their role in clearing the obstacles and helping youth find their way.

# Long-Term Missions (5+ Days)

## ORPHANAGE EXPERIENCE

*"Blessed are the merciful,*
*for they will be shown mercy. . . .*

*Rejoice and be glad, because great is your reward in heaven."*
*(Matthew 5:7-12a, NIV)*

**Project Description:** The youth will do repair work at an orphanage in a poverty-stricken area and give as much love to the orphans as they can for a few days. Each day, the teens will study and discuss the Beatitudes, which serve as the backdrop for the trip.

**Destination:** Call your denomination's mission agencies to find orphanage destinations that fit your travel budget.

**Travel and Lodging:** Some orphanages have guest quarters where you can stay and live among the children, usually for a donation. If you are traveling outside the US, find out the current requirements regarding passports, identification cards, and birth certificates.

**Expenses:** Travel may be your largest expense. Lodging will most likely require some kind of donation. If you leave the States, purchase a temporary visa for each person and additional insurance for any automobiles you take across a border. Have the teens' parents sign a notarized letter granting you guardianship and permission to take each minor out of the country on your specific travel dates; see page 101 for an example.

If your mission project requires supplies that you can purchase near your destination, plan on infusing some money into the local economy. Regardless of where you go, buy several cases of bottled water and build extra money into your mission budget for needs that arise while you are at the worksite.

**Get the Whole Church Involved:** Contact the orphanage ahead of time to find out what current needs they have in addition to your main mission project. Do they need school supplies? shoes? blankets? Once you find out, have a collection drive at your church and take those extra items with you.

If you can find out the number of boys and girls at the orphanage, personalize gift packages for each child. Have members of your church "adopt" a child and put together a package for him or her. Take the packages with you, and deliver them to the children.

## PREPARATION

If you go to Mexico, learn to speak common Spanish words and phrases. Your group probably has teens who take Spanish at school. Have them create a one-sheet reference page with English-to-Spanish words and phrases for the group to learn. Or they could create flash cards for practice.

For the more fluent Spanish speakers, have them practice reading children's stories so that they can read to the children at the orphanage.

If you are doing a building project or repairs, have the youth learn and practice the necessary techniques. Attending workshops would be especially helpful for construction work.

Invite your church to pray for the mission team and the children they will meet at the orphanage. Pray that the teens' example will reflect God's love and that they will pass that love to everyone they encounter. Pray that the youth will come to a new understanding of the Beatitudes. Ask God to keep the students safe as they travel and while they are at the worksite.

Does your church have a people who love to sew? If it does, ask them to make a nail apron for each member of the mission team. These gifts make great souvenirs from a life-changing mission experience.

To prepare for the cultural differences, gather as a mission team and talk about the conditions you are likely to experience, as well as cultural norms and daily life. As a group, study area to which you are headed, including the history of the area, the main industry, and poverty situation.

# SAMPLE SCHEDULE

Your schedule will vary according to the projects. Just be sure to build in time for your youth to play with the children. Begin each morning with personal prayer time in silence. Close every night with reflection on the day's experience, the corresponding discussion questions, and prayer.

Days 1–2       Travel, arrival, and settling

Day 3          On site; Blessed Are the Poor in Spirit questions (below)

Day 4          On site; Blessed Are Those Who Mourn questions (page 62)

Day 5          On site; Blessed Are the Meek questions (pages 62–63)

Day 6          On site; Blessed Are Those Who Hunger and Thirst for Righteousness (pages 63)

Day 7          On site; Blessed Are the Merciful questions (pages 63–64)

Day 8          On site; Blessed Are the Peacemakers questions (page 64)

Day 9          On site; Blessed Are Those Who Are Persecuted Because of Righteousness questions (page 65)

Day 10         Travel back home

Day 11         Travel and arrival

# DISCUSSION QUESTIONS

## Day 3: Blessed Are the Poor in Spirit

→ What has been the most unexpected thing to ever happen to you? Why was it unexpected?

→ How do you react when something unexpected happens?

→ In what ways did Jesus do the unexpected? (With whom did he eat?)

→ Many of Jesus' sayings run contrary to the expectations of the world. How do the Beatitudes fit in that category?

→ Read **Matthew 5:3**. What does being "poor in spirit" mean? Does Jesus want us to have nothing spiritually?

➡ What does a life of faith that always yearns for more of the Holy Spirit look like?

➡ Why might the kingdom of heaven be for the poor in spirit? How is this saying unexpected?

➡ How are you "poor in spirit"—or how are you not? How can you yearn for God more deeply this week?

## Day 4: Blessed Are Those Who Mourn

➡ What's the difference between mourning and being sad?

➡ When have you mourned? How were you comforted—or were you?

➡ **Read Matthew 5:4.** What does the word *comforted* mean? Can it mean strengthening in addition to consolation?

➡ How is Jesus' promise of comfort different from earthly comfort?

➡ How does Jesus' comfort make you stronger in faith?

➡ What type of great things could you do for God if you were strengthened spiritually?

➡ How are you doing great things for God this week?

## Day 5: Blessed Are the Meek

➡ What is the difference between *meek* and *weak*?

➡ Is it good to be meek? Why, or why not?

➡ What does the world think of meek people? Would you vote for a meek person to be President of the United States? Why, or why not?

➡ Read **Matthew 5:5.** Jesus says the meek will inherit the earth. How does this promise differ from the world's idea of who will end up on top?

➔ When do we see Jesus being meek?

➔ The world says rich, famous, greedy, and cut-throat people win or succeed; but Jesus said the humble will win in the end. So, is it possible to be meek and succeed in our world? Explain.

➔ Are you meek? How has this mission trip humbled you?

## Day 6: Blessed Are Those Who Hunger and Thirst for Righteousness

➔ When have you been famished? Do you get thirsty on the worksite? How does it feel when you finally get a drink of water?

➔ When do you feel the most full? After Thanksgiving or Christmas dinner? How does smelling food cooking before you eat compare to how you feel after getting to eat?

➔ Read **Matthew 5:6**. Do you hunger and thirst for righteousness? Are you filled?

➔ When do we see Jesus hunger and thirst for righteousness?

➔ What do people think or say about other people who are looking to be filled spiritually?

➔ Do people who are "filled" act differently than others? If so, how? If no, why not?

➔ Are you searching for righteousness? How?

➔ How can you increase your appetite for righteousness?

## Day 7: Blessed Are the Merciful

➔ Read **Matthew 5:7**. What's the difference between mercy and justice?

➔ Do you use mercy when dealing with people, or do you use justice?

➔ Do you want God to use mercy when judging you? How?

→ When do we see Jesus being merciful?

→ Why, do you think, did Jesus talk a lot about grace and mercy?

→ Why is mercy a godly quality?

→ What does society think of the quality of mercy? Is it a good thing, or a sign of weakness? Why?

→ How are you going to show mercy tomorrow? next week? next month?

→ What situation in your life have you been approaching from a justice view that you need to switch to a mercy view?

## Day 8: Blessed Are the Peacemakers

→ When have you been in conflict with someone? How did you handle it?

→ **Read Matthew 5:9.** What does being a peacemaker mean?

→ At what times was Jesus a peacemaker?

→ How can you be a peacemaker when you're one of the parties involved in the conflict?

→ How can you be a peacemaker when the conflict involves two of your friends?

→ How can you be a peacemaker when the conflict involves groups of people?

→ Other than healing relationships between people, how can a peacemaker help bring peace to an individual? (Answers may include helping someone resolve lingering pain caused by a negative experience.)

→ Where do you feel God calling you to be a peacemaker?

→ What specific action are you going to take to bring peace to a broken or stressed relationship in your life?

## Day 9: Blessed Are Those Who Are Persecuted Because of Righteousness

→ What people are famous for standing up for their beliefs?

→ Tell us about a time when you had to stand up for your beliefs. How did others treat you? Were you supported, or criticized?

→ Read **Matthew 5:10.** Have you ever been persecuted because of your faith? Was the persecution from others who also believe in God, or was it from non-believers?

→ When was Jesus persecuted because of righteousness?

→ Why did Jesus say we should be glad and rejoice when we are persecuted because of him? What's so great about being made fun of, attacked, or killed on behalf of God?

→ What does "for theirs is the kingdom of heaven" mean?

→ How do you keep from "fighting back" when you're under attack?

→ How can you support others when they are being persecuted?

## FOLLOW-UP

Have the youth organize photos and make memory books of the mission. Each month, post a photo of one of the children from the orphanage and ask the youth to write a paragraph about that child. Or show the photo and ask youth to recall any interaction they had with that child.

Host a slide show of your trip, showing photos of the work you did onsite. Include photos of youth interacting with the children at the orphanage.

Challenge your church to continue supporting the orphanage through offering collections, prayers, donation of items and ongoing mission trips to the worksite.

# FIND YOUR BEARING

*The fruit of the Spirit is love, joy, peace, patience, kindness, generosity, faithfulness, gentleness, and self-control. There is no law against such things.*

*(Galatians 5:22-23)*

**Project Description:** Your youth will volunteer at your church's children's vacation Bible school program and then take it on the road. They will have already taught it and learned the crafts and songs, so go and share the love!

**Destination and Duration:** You could do an inner-city program in your area or go as far as Mexico. Think about your budget and what your group is ready for. You might offer a VBS to a church that doesn't have the volunteers or finances to host a one. This mission will take five days plus travel.

**Travel, Expenses, and Lodging:** The cost of this trip will depend on how far you travel, the extensiveness of the vacation Bible school program, and how many youth participate. Arrange to stay at the church or community center where you are hosting the VBS. If you can't stay at the same location, stay at another church or a hotel; just remember to include in your budget the added expense of a hotel.

Each day of VBS, include lunch for all the participants. The cost will depend on where you go and how many children you estimate will attend.

**Get the Whole Church Involved:** If the mission site is near your home church, recruit congregation members to help teach VBS classes. Before the trip, enlist the VBS teachers and organizers from your church to pass on their wisdom and guidance to the team developing the mission. Get everyone involved by setting up a collection bin at your church and encouraging donations of supplies needed for the mission, such as pencils and paper.

## PREPARATION

Ask the students to memorize **Galatians 5:22-23,** so that they are familiar with the fruits of the Spirit before the mission. Talk about how, through leading VBS, they will practice "bearing fruit." They will share the gospel through the program, but pray that the Spirit would work in your youth to bear fruit.

Connect your youth to the VBS coordinator at your church to make sure that they are all signed up as volunteers. Collect all of the used teacher books for the youth to use on the mission. Order additional VBS resources.

Invite your church to pray for the mission team and the children who will attend the VBS. Pray that the youth will allow themselves to be nurtured and cultivated as they explore the fruits of the Spirit.

Have some youth create a devotion booklet focusing one fruit for each page. Distribute the booklets to all participants in the two weeks leading up to the mission.

Train the mission team on how to teach to little children. This training should include skills and techniques for keeping little ones focused and occupied.

## SAMPLE THEME SCHEDULE

Most vacation Bible school programs last four to five days. Choose the appropriate number of fruits of the Spirit to match the number of days for your program.

| | |
|---|---|
| **Day 1** | Travel to destination |
| **Day 2** | Onsite: Love and Joy (pages 68–69) |
| **Day 3** | Onsite: Peace and Patience (page 69) |
| **Day 4** | Onsite: Kindness and Goodness (page 69–70) |
| **Day 5** | Onsite: Faithfulness and Gentleness (page 70) |
| **Day 6** | Onsite: Self-control and Wrap-Up (page 71) |
| **Day 7** | Return home |

## SAMPLE DAILY SCHEDULE

| | |
|---|---|
| 8:00 A.M. | Rise and shine |
| 8:30 A.M. | Devotion and worship |
| 9:00 A.M. | Breakfast |
| 10:00 A.M. | VBS begins |

| 12:00 P.M. | Lunch |
| 12:30 P.M. | VBS kids leave |
| 1:00 P.M. | Clean up and prepare for the next day |
| 2:00 P.M. | Work around the host church (yardwork, vacuum, dust) |
| 4:00 P.M. | Free time |
| 6:00 P.M. | Dinner |
| 6:45 P.M. | Free time |
| 7:30 P.M. | Discussion Questions in small groups. (See below; for each day, choose the corresponding set of questions.) |
| 8:30 P.M. | Evening worship and reflection |
| 9:30 P.M. | Free time |
| 10:30 P.M. | Brush and flush |
| 11:30 P.M. | Lights out |

## DISCUSSION QUESTIONS

### Day 1: Love and Joy

➔ What's your favorite fruit?

➔ Where do fruits come from?

➔ If a tree or plant produces a fruit, what is a fruit of the Spirit? Why are they called fruits?

➔ What are some things you love? Why?

➔ How is love different from really liking something? In reality, do you love ice cream, or do you just really like it?

➔ How is God's definition of love *(agape)* different from the ones we use—romantic love *(eros)* and friendship or brotherly love *(philios)*?

→ Is loving the way God wants easy, or difficult? Why?

→ Was it easy to demonstrate God's love today at VBS? Why, or why not?

→ What is the difference between joy and just being happy?

→ Why does God want us to have joy and share joy?

→ Have you experienced joy today? If so, when? What made you feel joy?

→ What's in the way? What's keeping you from bearing love and joy?

→ What are you asking God to do in you to cultivate love and joy?

## Day 2: Peace and Patience

→ When is a time you felt most at peace?

→ What does *peace* mean? What is God's definition of *peace*? How does that idea compare to our world's definition of *peace*?

→ Who is bringing peace to you? How?

→ How are you bringing peace to those you worked with today?

→ Why is patience a fruit of the Spirit?

→ How is patience different from waiting?

→ Where do you see patience in your life? Where do you need patience?

→ What's keeping you from bearing peace and patience?

→ What are you asking God to do in your life to cultivate them?

## Day 3: Kindness and Goodness

→ When has someone you didn't know been kind to you?

→ How has someone shown kindness today? How have you done so today?

→ How can you make kindness a way of life, not just an act or gesture?

→ What is the difference between being good and goodness?

→ What is so important about goodness that it would be a fruit of the Spirit?

→ What is one way you can act out of goodness this week? when you return home after the mission? for a lifetime?

→ What is keeping you from bearing kindness and goodness? What are you asking God to do in your life to cultivate them?

## Day 4: Faithfulness and Gentleness

→ What does the word *faithful* mean? Who in your life has demonstrated faithfulness?

→ How does trust fit in with faithfulness? What other words can be used to describe faithfulness? (Answers may include *loyalty* and *dependability*.)

→ How is faithfulness different from having faith?

→ How can Christians demonstrate faithfulness to others? to God?

→ When you hear the word *gentleness,* what do you think of? Is that idea what gentleness means as a fruit of the Spirit? If so, why? If no, then what does it mean?

→ What is the opposite of gentleness? (Answers may include harshness, bluntness, being critical, anger, insensitivity, and not understanding.)

→ When has someone used gentleness with you? Did you appreciate it? Why, or why not?

→ How have you acted with gentleness on this mission—or have you?

→ What is keeping you from bearing faithfulness and gentleness?

→ What are you asking God to do in your life to cultivate them?

## Day 5: Self-Control and Wrap-up

➡ When have you used self-control? What would have happened if you hadn't used it?

➡ When was a time when you wish someone else had used self-control with you?

➡ Does self-control benefit you, others, or both? How?

➡ What is the hardest thing about using self-control? Why?

➡ What is keeping you from bearing self-control? What are you asking God to do in your life to cultivate self-control?

**Wrap up your discussion on fruits of the Spirit by asking these questions:**

➡ What are some of the things all of the fruits of the Spirit have in common?

➡ Compare the fruits of the Spirit with the "world's way." What do you notice? (The fruits of the Spirit are opposite to the ways of the world.) What does that comparison tell you about God and how we should live as Christians?

➡ What does **Galatians 5:23** mean when it says, "there is no law against such things"?

➡ Using the analogy of fruit, what do we now know about the fruits of the Spirit? How do we grow them? How are they planted? How do they bring refreshment and nourishment?

➡ Which of the fruits of the Spirit is hardest for you? Which is easiest? Which do you wish you had more of?

➡ What have you learned about yourself and the fruit you bear? Have you found that you had some fruits you weren't aware of? Have you discovered you didn't have as much of a fruit as you thought you had?

➡ What are you going to ask God to do to help you cultivate these fruits of the Spirit? Does one stand out above the others as one you are going to start with? If so, which one? Why?

## FOLLOW-UP

In the months following the mission, bring a bowl or platter of fruit to youth group. Designate a fruit of the Spirit to actual fruit you've brought. For example, kiwis could represent love; apples, goodness; and grapes, self-control. Have the youth take pieces of fruit then talk about how they are doing with the specific fruits of the Spirit.

Send to the students postcards or notecards shaped like pieces of fruit, along with a note of support and encouragement.

Here are two options for following up with supporters of the mission:

➜ Have a continental breakfast at church one morning before, after, or between worship services, serving lots of fruit. Ask the youth who participated in the mission to interact with supporters at the meal and tell stories from the trip.

➜ Invite supporters to a fondue dessert where they can dip fruit into chocolates and hear about the students' experience.

# BUILDING HOPE DURING TOUGH TIMES

*My brothers and sisters, whenever you face trials of any kind, consider it nothing but joy, because you know that the testing of your faith produces endurance; and let endurance have its full effect, so that you may be mature and complete, lacking in nothing.*

(James 1:2-4)

**Project Description:** Take the youth to a poverty-stricken area either in the US or abroad, and do a building project. Your denominational mission agency can direct you to a location; or look to mission programs such as Mountain TOP and Appalachian Service Project. Help the youth see that God is not absent from the lives of impoverished persons and that the youth can work to help meet basic needs.

**Destination and Duration:** A poverty-stricken area; five days or more

**Travel, Cost, and Lodging:** Depending on your destination, travel may be a major expense. If you don't want to spend all of your money on travel, research your area for projects that could make a difference locally. Your youth may not realize that how widespread poverty is.

Building and project supplies may be the bulk of your expense as well. Consult a contractor or other professional builder to plan for enough materials to finish your project; add extra money in the budget to cover overages. To save money, solicit sponsorships from hardware stores or other businesses in the community where you are working. Arrange to stay at a church, school, or community center near the worksite.

**Get the Whole Church Involved:** Beyond fundraising support, encourage the church to fast for a day or to live simply (not going out to movies and so on) while the youth are on the mission trip.

## PREPARATION

Study the area you are headed to. What is the history of the region? What hardships are the people facing? Have they been hit by unemployment or a natural disaster? Is there a lack of hope in the community?

Encourage the church to pray for the trip and for the safety of the youth as they work with tools. Also pray for the building that youth will work on, that it will help those who enter into it.

Study **James 1:2-4** to get a start on the main theme for the mission. Follow up with a look at people in the Bible who had to face hardships and trials, such as Joseph in **Genesis 37**. Other possibilities include Daniel, Jesus, Paul, Shadrach, Meshach, and Abendigo.

Practice basic building techniques, and provide building plans for the projects you'll be doing on the mission.

Go over what the youth can expect to see when they reach the worksite. And provide some training for appropriate ways of reacting to what they see without being judgmental or insulting.

## SAMPLE SCHEDULE

### Day 1: Travel and Arrival at the Destination

Days 2–6 : On site

Day 7: Travel and arrive back home

### Schedule Onsite, Days 2–6

| | |
|---|---|
| 6:30 A.M. | Rise and shine |
| 7:00 A.M. | Breakfast, make lunches |
| 8:00 A.M. | Leave for work project |
| 8:30 A.M. | Work project |
| 12:00 P.M. | Lunch at work project |
| 12:30 P.M. | Work project |
| 3:00 P.M. | Clean up, prepare for the following day |
| 3:30 P.M. | Leave work project |
| 4:00 P.M. | Shower, clean up, and free time |
| 6:00 P.M. | Dinner |
| 6:45 P.M. | Free time |
| 8:00 P.M. | Evening program (See the discussion questions.) |

| 9:00 P.M. | Small-group debriefing |
| 10:00 P.M. | Free time |
| 10:30 P.M. | Brush and flush |
| 11:00 P.M. | Lights out |

# DISCUSSION QUESTIONS

## Day 2: Trials and Hardships

➜ Why do bad things happen to good people? Have you ever asked that question? Any insights?

➜ What are some trials or hardships people face? What are some that you've personally faced?

➜ How do people typically react when they face trials and hardships?

➜ According to **James 1:2-4**, trials and hardships are a good thing. Is that Scripture true? Why, or why not?

➜ Why do we think that once we become a Christian, bad things won't happen anymore? Does God ever give us that promise?

➜ Why is there so much hardship in our world?

➜ How does your faith affect the way you face trials and hardships?

➜ Do you feel closer to God during tough times? Or do you feel abandoned by God?

Read or tell the popular poem "Footprints in the Sand" (which you can find on the Internet.)

Then ask:

➜ Could you be the man in the story? Do you feel like God isn't there for you when in reality you have pulled away?

➜ How can having Christian friends help you when you face hardships?

## Day 3: Hope

→ Have you ever hoped for something? Tell us about it.

→ What does hope look like? Describe it.

→ Have you ever felt like all hope was gone? When?

→ Contrast hope and hopelessness.

→ Is it hard or easy for you to have hope when you're facing trials? Why?

→ Where can you turn when you start to feel like you're losing hope?

→ What role does God play in your having hope?

→ What role do Christian friends play in your holding on to hope in the midst of challenging times?

→ What do you think it's like for people who don't have God or Christian friends in their life when they face trials and hardships?

→ Have you met people around this mission site who have hope? How do you think they can have hope in such poverty?

## Day 4: Perseverance

→ What are some synonyms for *perseverance*?

→ What is one of the hardest situations you've ever had to persevere?

→ Are you better off for having persevered? Why? Are you stronger? more mature?

→ How does hope relate to perseverance?

→ Why wouldn't it be better just to have an easy life all the time?

→ How does the testing of your faith develop perseverance? (Testing leads to a stronger faith, and a stronger faith holds on to hope and is more likely to persevere when things get tough.)

→ What does having a stronger or more mature faith mean?

→ What role does God play in helping you to persevere? What role do friends and family play?

→ How is perseverance working in you so that you may be mature and complete, not lacking anything?

## Day 5: Mature Faith

→ Have you ever said to someone or heard someone say to you, "Grow up" or "Act your age"? What is the difference between being mature and being grown up?

→ Who is the most mature person you know? Why?

→ What is a mature faith?

→ How has this trip helped your faith mature?

→ What does your faith lack? What's missing? What needs growing to give you a mature faith?

→ Are you ready and willing to ask God for perseverance so that your faith may be matured and complete, lacking in nothing? What might that entail?

→ What are some other important elements to maturing your faith? How do Bible study, youth group, worship, and missions factor into your maturing?

## Day 6: Joy

→ What brings you joy? Why?

→ How are joy and happiness the same? different?

→ Have your parents ever said, "We just want you to be happy"? Why don't we ever say, "I just want you to be joyful"?

→ Are tough times ever joyful? Why, or why not?

→ Can joy be found in the response to tough times? How? (There is often great joy found in the response to disasters such as famine, flood, or fire; the joy comes from people giving of themselves to help recovery and rebuilding.)

→ How does joy help you get through the tough times?

→ Does God bring you joy? If so, how? If no, why not?

→ How can you share your joy with others?

## FOLLOW-UP

Collect enough nails from the worksite to make crosses for each member of your mission team. Bind the nails together with a thin gauge wire; wrap it around the nails to hold them in place. A month after returning from your mission, mail each youth a cross along with a short note reminding him or her of the trip. Let the students know that the cross is made from nails used in building hope on the mission.

Follow up on a one-on-one basis with each participant, asking them how they are doing at letting perseverance mature their faith.

Talk about your experiences from the trip; then encourage the congregation to support further ongoing work in that community. Provide a specific way for them to donate money to be used for a specific cause in that community.

# THE WORLD: NATURALLY IT'S GOOD!

*In the beginning God created the heavens and the earth. Now the earth was formless and empty, darkness was over the surface of the deep, and the Spirit of God was hovering over the waters. And God said, "Let there be light," and there was light.*

*(Genesis 1:1-2:3, NIV)*

**Project Description:** Work with an environmental group, and take your youth to care for God's creation. You might work on natural-disaster clean-up, oil spills, forest replanting, trail building, or a wildlife refuge; just find a project your group will get excited about, and go for it.

**Destination and Duration:** A state or national forest or natural area; about five days plus travel time

**Travel, Cost, and Lodging:** You might have to travel quite a ways to get to an area that needs forest replanting. If you stay in tents, you'll need to pay for a camping permit and any park fees.

Camping will still be less expensive than a hotel or lodge. Otherwise, plan on normal expenses such as travel and food.

**Ideas for Saving Money:** If a church, lodge, or retreat center is not near your worksite, consider making this trip a camping excursion. Sleep in tents, and stay in an area close to where you are doing your work. Staying in the outdoors will enhance your look at creation as you serve God.

See what kind of resources (such as tents, cooking stoves, and sleeping bags) church members or any scouting groups your church sponsors are willing to offer. You'll save a bunch of money by borrowing supplies as opposed to buying them.

**Get the Whole Church Involved:** Pray that the mission team would have a greater appreciation for our environment and all of God's creation.

Pray for the planet and our natural resources; and pray that God would help us to be good stewards of the creation entrusted to our care.

Try these fundraising ideas to involve the whole church:

➜ Organize a plant sale, recruiting the green thumbs from your church to help.

➜ Have a buy-an-acre sale, where church members can buy the seedlings for an acre of land. Find out how many seedlings are required for an acre of forest and how much seedlings cost. Come up with the total, and sell acres (or half acres). If it's too expensive for one person, encourage people to go in together on an acre.

## PREPARATION

Provide some environmental education for the youth and adult sponsors. Talk about how ecosystems work and how an impact on one area affects all of the related areas. Some people don't realize that their piece of litter starts a chain reaction that leads back to humans. This concept has revealed itself in areas where polluted water from washing cars runs off into the water where, small organisms and small fish eat the pollution then larger fish eat the smaller fish. The larger fish are caught and served to humans, so we're eating the same pollution that we washed off our cars.

Have the supporters create a photo devotion book or journal for youth. It should include photos of nature along with devotions and thoughts about creation. You can use this as a journal too by including a blank page or two with every photo. Then the youth can record their experiences, thoughts, and prayers while on the mission.

Study the Creation stories in **Genesis 1** and **Genesis 2**, exploring one day of Creation at a time.

Ask:

➜ What is significant about the order in which things were created?

➜ What was God's reaction to each day and night's creation?

## SAMPLE SCHEDULE

**Day 1:** Travel to the worksite

**Day 2–4:** Work onsite

**Day 5:** Travel home

### Work site schedule, Days 2-4

|  |  |
|---|---|
| 8:00 A.M. | Rise and shine |
| 9:00 A.M. | Breakfast |
| 9:30 A.M. | Leave base camp |
| 10:00 A.M. | Work project |
| 12:30 P.M. | Lunch |
| 1:00 P.M. | Work Project |
| 4:00 P.M. | Small-group discussion (See the discussion questions below.) |
| 5:00 P.M. | Return to base camp |
| 6:00 P.M. | Dinner |
| 7:00 P.M. | Free time |
| 9:00 P.M. | Campfire |
| 10:30 P.M. | Brush and flush (if you're lucky enough to have running water!) |
| 11:00 P.M. | Lights out |

## DISCUSSION QUESTIONS

To enhance your mission, enlist an environmental specialist to accompany your group for the week. This person may be a former or current park ranger, college professor, member of an environmental advocacy group, or a pastor with a passion for earth ministries. Even an earth-science student could share information on watersheds and ecosystems.

## Day 1: The Gift of Creation

→ What is one of your all-time favorite gifts that you've given to someone? Why?

→ Do you think God feels the same way about giving us the gift of creation?

→ How would you define *creation*?

→ How is all of creation—people, nature, animals, plants—a gift?

→ What part of creation do you tend to forget about? (Answers may include underwater life, outer space, and polar caps.)

→ Which part of creation do you appreciate most?

→ Which part of creation might you take advantage of without realizing it?

→ How do you share the gift of creation with others?

→ How do you share the gift of creation with God, the Creator?

→ Have you sent a thank-you note to God for the gift of creation? If so, how? If no, why not?

## Day 2: God in Creation

→ Where is one of your favorite places to vacation? Why?

→ When do you feel closest to God? Why?

→ Why do people feel closest to God amongst creation and outdoors?

→ Where do you see God in nature? If you don't, why not?

→ Why do you think God created such a complex, beautiful gift with such variety? Does it blow your mind that new species of plants and animals are discovered all the time?

→ Looking at creation, we get a glimpse into who God is and what God looks like. What have you learned about God from creation?

→ What does God's limitless creativity in nature tell us about ourselves as creations of God?

→ Does that message change the way you view others? yourself? How?

→ How do you celebrate that variety and diversity of God's creation?

## Day 3: Human Impact

→ Tell us about one of your most amazing outdoor memories. What made it so special?

→ What are some of the ways we humans impact creation? Think of positive ways as well as negative.

→ How might have you made a destructive impact on creation without realizing it?

→ How, other than on the mission this week, have you personally made a positive impact on creation?

→ What are some of the consequences or effects on creation resulting from the destructive impact we make on creation?

→ What is the impact on us as humans when we don't properly care for creation?

→ In **Genesis 1:26-30**, God creates humans to be stewards, or caretakers, of what has been created. What are you doing in your role as steward to take care of creation? If you aren't doing anything, why not?

## Day 4: Caring for God's Creation

→ What is one of the most valuable (monetary or sentimental) gifts you have ever received? Why was it so important to you? Did you take care of it? Do you still have the gift? Why, or why not?

→ How do we treat the gift of creation with respect?

→ What does being a good steward mean?

➜ What are some easy things you can do in your everyday life to care for creation? (Answers may include not littering, as well as walking or riding a bike instead of driving.)

➜ Let's create a list of small things our youth group can do to care for creation. (Answers may include carpooling to youth group and recycling aluminum cans, paper, and glass.)

➜ How can we be God's partner in caring for creation?

➜ Do you have a new appreciation for our world because of the work you've done this week? Why, or why not?

## OPTION

Arrange to visit a national park or other amazing natural landmark in transit to or from your mission site. You may want to add an additional day to the itinerary to give you enough time to take in the extra peek at God's creation.

## FOLLOW-UP

Give a pine cone to each participant as a reminder of that person's work and his or her responsibility as a steward of creation. Attach a note asking about the progress each youth is having with doing the "little things" to help protect the environment. If you planted deciduous trees instead of coniferous trees, collect some leaves and give them instead of pine cones.

If you're planting in a forest, save one seedling to be planted on church grounds when you return. Check with your church for proper placement.

Give a report to your congregation, telling the people how many seedlings were planted and how many years it will take for the seedlings to grow. Use average year-to-height numbers, saying, for example, "In five years, the trees we planted will be seven feet tall. And in ten years, the trees will be twenty feet tall." This kind of estimate will give them an idea of the time required to replace a natural resource they use every day.

Another way to follow up with supporters is to start a recycling program at your church. Provide recycle bins at key locations in your church, and encourage the members to use them.

Part of the recycling program is bins, but the other part is reusing rather than throwing away. For example, use the blank side of misprinted copy paper to receive faxes, or cut it into sheets to be used for taking messages and writing notes.

Hand out "Reduce, Reuse, Recycle" stickers along with a fact sheet and ideas for things people can do around the house to help the environment.

# GOOD SPORTS

*The body is a unit, though it is made up of many parts; and though all its parts are many, they form one body. So it is with Christ.*
*(1 Corinthians 12:12, NIV)*

**Project Description:** This mission is all about sharing the good news of God's love. The youth will develop their personal testimonies and share them while hosting athletic clinics, workshops, and games for children.

**Destination and Duration:** Any location; three to five days, plus additional days for travel

**Travel, Cost, and Lodging:** You will have all of the normal expenses associated with a mission; but depending on your destination, your costs could go way up, especially if you decide to fly somewhere. You'll also have the expenses of sports equipment and supplies such as uniforms and balls. To counteract this cost, have an equipment drive at church or see whether a local sports team has any used equipment they could donate.

For lodging, check out youth hostels, bed and breakfasts, hotels, churches, camps, and retreat centers. Churches or schools may be your best bet. Just make sure your sleep destination is near a park or field where the youth can play the sport they picked.

**Get the Whole Church Involved:** If your congregation has any current or former coaches, ask them to help with the preparation and implementation of the mission. They can share valuable insight about organizing and teaching the workshops and games for children.

If your mission site is close to your home church, invite congregation members to come and watch the games. Have them make signs and cheer for both sides.

## PREPARATION

This mission is a little different from other missions in this book because the main focus is more on street evangelism and personal testimonies.

If much of your group does not already play a sport, pick one to teach and play on the mission. Your destination may influence the sport, or vice versa.

Once you've chosen a sport and put a team together, have some practices so that the youth can become familiar with the game.

Once you're at the mission site, you'll provide workshops and set up games. Children and youth will play on each team. Remind your group that the object of the mission isn't to come home with an undefeated record; it's to engage others through sports and then share the message of Jesus Christ. So the teens need not be discouraged or have a bad attitude if their team loses.

After the games and workshops, you'll gather the teams and pray with them, giving thanks for the game and your new friends. Then the youth will spend some time hanging out, talking, and witnessing.

To prepare for the faith sharing, each participant should write out his or her testimony. This task will help the team members organize their thoughts and memorize more easily.

Having written the testimonies, the participants need to receive training in sharing their faith with others. Witnessing can be intimidating, especially to strangers. Practice sharing your testimonies by letting everyone speak in front of the group and lead prayer. If you're going to a foreign country where you'll use a translator, practice speaking one sentence at a time to get a feel for the staggered pace of delivery. Wait for a few moments in between each sentence or thought.

Have the youth write devotions based on various parts of the body of Christ (1 Corinthians 12:12-31). Compile these devotions, and create a booklet to be given to each participant while they're on the mission.

Pray for the mission team's travels and for injury-free competition. And most of all, pray for the witness of the youth as they compete and share the love of Christ. Pray for those who hear the message of Jesus' redeeming love and the hope that comes with knowing him.

## SAMPLE DAILY SCHEDULE

8:30 A.M.      Rise and shine

9:00 A.M.      Breakfast

10:30 A.M.     Skills clinic

12:30 P.M.     Lunch

| 1:30 P.M. | Small-group discussion questions (below) |
| 2:30 P.M. | Free time and faith sharing |
| 4:00 P.M. | Practice |
| 5:00 P.M. | Dinner |
| 6:30 P.M. | Game time |
| 8:30 P.M. | Hang out and faith sharing |
| 9:30 P.M. | Return home and clean-up |
| 11:00 P.M. | Lights out |

## SMALL-GROUP DISCUSSION QUESTIONS

### Day 1

➔ How many bones are there in the human body? (206 in an adult, 350 in an infant, which fuse as we grow) What is the biggest? (femur) What is the smallest? (the stirrup bone, or the stapes bone, in your middle ear)

➔ Have you ever hit your funny bone? How did it feel? That sensation is caused by a tiny nerve that runs close to the surface of your skin near your elbow. Are you surprised that something so small could create such a big sensation?

➔ What does 1 Corinthians 12:12-26 tell us about the parts of the body?

➔ How intentional do you think God was in designing our bodies? Why?

➔ Which part of your body would you least like to lose? Your legs? Arms? Nose? Eyes? Hands? Ears? Why?

➔ Which part of your body is most important to you—or do you not have a favorite?

➔ Why is the body so important to God? Regarding God's view of our bodies, what insight does 1 Corinthians 6:19-20 give us ?

## Day 2

→ Are you a competitive person? If so, give an example.

→ How do you handle losing?

→ So how do you feel about the idea that all parts of the body are equal?

→ If every part of the body needs every other part of the body to be complete, then what's your notion of winning or being better?

→ Do you feel that you need other parts of the body so that you can be the best you can? Why, or why not?

→ How do you think other parts of the body feel when you have to win and do whatever it takes, including disrespecting them?

→ How do you think God feels when you do so?

→ How can God help you have a healthier approach to competition?

## Day 3

→ What groups of people do you belong to? (Answers may include clubs, organizations, and family.)

→ What does *the body of Christ* mean?

→ If we think of the body of Christ as all of our Christian sisters and brothers—real people—how does our approach to competition change?

→ Go back and read through the previous day's questions; but this time replace the word *body* with *body of Christ.* Do you feel differently?

→ Is the body a good metaphor for the body of Christ? Why, or why not?

→ How can God help you in being a strong part of the body of Christ?

→ How can you, as part of the body, help other parts succeed?

→ How does **1 Corinthians 12:12** affect your attitude toward people who are different from you in one way or another?

## FOLLOW-UP

Encourage the participants to stay in touch with the children with whom they played. Bring a piece of equipment from the sport you played to youth group one night. (If you played baseball, bring a baseball.) Toss the ball to one of the participants, and ask that teen how he or she is running "in such a way as to get the prize" and training "to get a crown that will last forever" (**1 Corinthians 9:24-25**).

In your weekly church worship, take a few minutes each week for one youth to tell of his or her experience and lift up in prayer one person, one part of the body, he or she met on the mission.

# THE REAL WORLD

*And what does the LORD require of you?*
*To act justly and to love mercy*
*and to walk humbly with your God.*
                              *(Micah 6:8b)*

**Project Description:** This experience will expose the youth to the issue of global hunger and inspire them to work on behalf of impoverished persons after they return home.

**Destination and Duration:** Heifer Ranch in Perryville, Arkansas; three days, plus travel time

**Travel, Cost, and Lodging:** The two-days-and-nights Global Passport program costs $150 per person. The three-days-and-nights program costs $200 per person. These prices include food and lodging at the Ranch, but getting there will cost you additional money. A train or plane into Little Rock might work well, but you'll have to rent vehicles to get out to the Heifer Ranch. When you are not staying in the Global Village, the open-air bunk barn is available at the Ranch and is included in the registration fee.

**Note:** The Global Passport programs require a minimum of twenty participants and is open only to grades nine and up.

**Get the Whole Church Involved:** Encourage church members to become more aware of how much they use and waste. When the youth return home, they will have ideas that fit your context; support them and help execute their plans in the life of the church.

## PREPARATION

Before the trip, have the participants research living conditions and poverty levels around the globe, finding facts and figures on people who die from hunger and disease. Contact your state agency that deals with poverty, and find out the poverty level and median income for your area.

Ask area food banks how your group can volunteer.

Invite your church to pray that the youth have their eyes opened and grasp the severity of the problem. Pray that the teens be moved to a lifetime of action helping to eliminate poverty and hunger in the world.

Unlike the other mission ideas in this book, Global Passport is a plug-and-play, which takes care of the programming. And rather than having the youth directly helping people on the trip, it focuses on educating and empowering participants to return to their local church and community to effect change in others. Your initial reaction might be, "But what do we get to build?" or "When do we witness to the locals?" The truth is that this powerful experience will build an understanding of global issues in your youth, and those in your church will witness a transformation in the youth who participate. This investment in your mission ministry will pay off for years to come!

## About Heifer® International

Heifer International is a nonprofit organization started in 1944 that works to end world hunger and poverty by providing struggling families with farm animals and livestock. Here's how the concept works: Families receive an animal and training on how to use the animal to provide food or clothing for the family. They, in turn, pass along an offspring of the animal to another needy person or family. Heifer offers opportunities to purchase animals for needy families. You can even buy a package of bees complete with beehives to help pollinate crops, leading to higher production. Visit *heifer.org* to learn more.

## About Heifer Ranch

Heifer Ranch is a 1,200 acre, hands-on learning center located in Perryville, Arkansas, forty-five miles northwest of Little Rock. The Ranch focuses on promoting sustainable solutions for world hunger and poverty. The two other Heifer learning centers are located in California and Massachusetts.

Heifer Ranch offers a wide variety of programs for all age groups starting with pre-kindergarden. Youth in grade six and up have several options ranging from half-day to five-day programs. Heifer Ranch hosts over 28,000 visitors each year as they educate people about the root causes and solutions to poverty and hunger around the globe. Call (501) 889-524 for more information.

## About Global Passport (Grades 9 and Above)

The Global Passport program gives your youth a taste of the real world. Participants are given an orientation on how the village operates and what will be expected of them during their stay. "Villagers" as they're called, are divided into "family" units, given resources, and sent to one of the homes in the village. Homes range from a refugee tent camp to a three-bedroom Guatemalan house with cement floor. The youth might stay in a Tibetan yurt made of yak hair, a Thai stilt house made of bamboo, a Ugandan house made of homemade bricks, an Appalachian house, or the urban slums, where houses are made out of wood scraps. During their stay, "villagers" must negotiate with other "families" for resources such as water, food, and firewood.

Global Passport will expose youth to the realities of poverty and hunger and open their eyes to the drastic conditions many people face every day.

**Note:** Global Gateway is a one-night, less intensive program for sixth graders and up.

### About Service Programs

Service Programs are offered only at Summer Action and Alternative Spring Break times. The programs offer various workshops and activities to help participants better understand the global issues associated with hunger and poverty. Your group will be mixed with other groups from around the country as you actively tackle service projects (such as painting, repair, and maintenance) at the Ranch.

During your week-long adventure, your sessions will include experiential learning, as well as service opportunities. A highlight of the week is a night in the Global Village with your new community.

## SCHEDULE

Global Passport (three nights) runs Sunday evening through Wednesday mid-morning or Thursday evening through Sunday mid-morning.

Global Passport (four nights) runs Monday evening through Friday mid-morning.

## FOLLOW-UP

Because the programming will be done for you, put more effort into the debriefing and application back home.

Start collecting an offering at youth group, and as a group use the money to purchase animals through Heifer. Keep a tally on the youth bulletin board of what's been provided, or, set a goal of providing an entire flock. Put a flock of paper animals up in the youth room, coloring each one in as money is raised and animals are purchased. This visual reminder will help track their progress.

Develop a culture of careful consideration as the teens improve their stewardship of resources such as food and money.

Encourage your congregation to give the gift of an animal through Heifer International rather than giving gifts of "stuff."

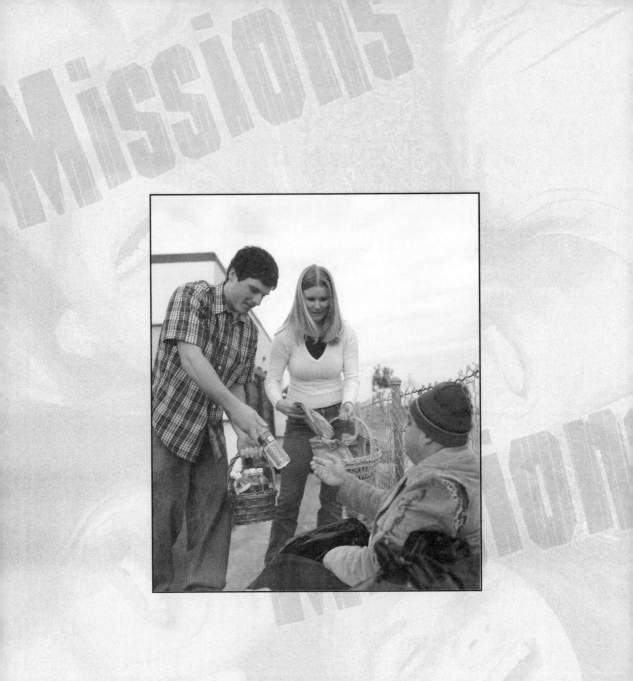

**Ready to Go** →

# Sample Pages and Reproducible Forms

## INDEX OF FORMS

# COST-ESTIMATION SAMPLE

## Cost-per-Person Breakdown

$400.00   plug-and-play registration

| | |
|---|---|
| $125.00 | building materials, project supplies |
| $120.00 | staff and program costs |
| $ 80.00 | lodging |
| $ 75.00 | food |
| $400.00 | total plug-and-play registration |

$325.00   airfare
$ 79.36   van rental

$992 to rent a van
x   2 vans
$$\frac{\$1{,}984}{25 \text{ people}} = \$79.36 \text{ per person}$$

$ 18.00   fuel

$$\frac{900 \text{ mi}}{12 \text{ mpg}} = 75 \text{ gal needed} \times \frac{\$3}{\text{gal}} = \$225$$

$$\times \quad 2 \text{ vans}$$

$$\frac{\$450}{25 \text{ people}} = \$18 \text{ per person}$$

$ 30.00   water-park fun day
$ 20.00   food (4 meals, $5 each)
$ 25.00   additional lodging and food
**$897.36   total cost per person**

**$897.36 x 25 people = $22,434**

# PARENT HANDOUT

### Senior High Mission Trip, July 1–July 9, 2006
### Hurricane Katrina Recovery, New Orleans, Louisiana

## Cost-per-Person Breakdown

$400.00   workcamp registration

| | |
|---|---|
| $125.00 | building materials, project supplies |
| $120.00 | staff and program costs |
| $ 80.00 | lodging |
| $ 75.00 | food |
| $400.00 | total workcamp registration |

$325.00   airfare

$ 79.36   van rental

$992 to rent a van and trailer

x   2 vans

$1,984/25 people  =  $79.36 per person

$ 18.00   fuel

$900 \text{ mi}/12 \text{ mpg} = 75$ gal needed  x  $3/\text{gal}$ = $225

x   2 vans

$450/25 people = $18 per person

$ 30.00   water park

$ 45.00   additional lodging and food

$897.36   **total cost per person***

21 people from Edmonds UMC  =  $18,844.56

+  4 people from partner church  =   $3,589.44

**25 people going for a total of        $22,434.00**

*Additional expenses include tools, respirator, and spending money.

## Itinerary

July 1: Depart from Seattle at 11:40 A.M., arrive at Houston at 5:56 P.M.

July 2: Drive to New Orleans, depart at 7:00 A.M., arrive at 3:00 P.M.

July 7: Drive to Houston

July 8: Spend day at water park

July 9: Depart from Houston at 8:45 P.M., arrive at Seattle at 11:05 P.M.

# Sample of an Expenditures Log
## Senior High Mission, June 2006
## 17 Participants

### Fast food

| | | |
|---|---|---|
| $ | 80.35 | Burger King® (lunch) |
| $ | 90.97 | Lucky 13 Pizza (dinner) |
| $ | 54.15 | McDonald's (breakfast) |
| $ | 95.83 | Carl's Jr.® (lunch)—cash |
| $ | 135.50 | Moab Diner (dinner) |
| $ | 50.14 | City Market (breakfast) |
| $ | 77.43 | A&W (lunch) |
| $ | 78.89 | McDonald's (lunch) |
| $ | 107.72 | Denny's (dinner) |
| $ | 58.75 | Burger King® (Breakfast) |
| $ | 1.17 | Burger King® (breakfast)—cash |
| $ | 90.40 | Arby's® (lunch) |
| $ | 98.03 | Pizza Hut® (dinner) |
| $ | 59.13 | Albertsons (breakfast) |
| $ | 100.28 | Subway® (lunch) |
| $ 1,177.57 | | total food    ($1,700 budgeted) |

### Fuel

| | | |
|---|---|---|
| $ | 34.72 | Costco |
| $ | 113.07 | Shell |
| $ | 104.77 | Shell |
| $ | 122.79 | Albertsons |
| $ | 76.09 | Texico |
| $ | 123.86 | Red Mesa Express |
| $ | 61.18 | Red Mesa Express—cash |
| $ | 62.87 | K&C Trading Post |
| $ | 114.72 | North Rim Country Store |
| $ | 113.00 | Chevron |
| $ | 92.65 | Phillips 66® |
| $ | 109.02 | Shell |
| $ | 105.96 | Union 76 |
| $ 1,234.70 | | total fuel    ($1,600 budgeted) |

### Van Care, Supplies, and Miscellaneous

| | |
|---|---|
| $ 63.39 | Costco (atlas, first-aid kits, markers) |
| $ 150.02 | Wal-Mart (fans, 6 coolers) |
| $ 9.53 | Kmart (sun shades, gum) |
| $ 13.61 | Red Mesa Express (popsicles for youth) |
| $ 19.00 | Union 76 (2 van washes) |
| $ 296.36 | Home Depot (tools and supplies for worksites) |
| $ 551.91 | total van care, supplies, and miscellaneous  ($200 budgeted) |

## Photos, Souvenirs & Attractions

| | |
|---|---|
| $    6.41 | post cards and Kokopelli bandanna—cash |
| $  51.00 | Four Corners admittance—cash |
| $  32.00 | mini pots for adult thank-you gifts (3)—cash |
| $  20.00 | Grand Canyon National Park—cash |
| $  20.00 | Grand Canyon National Park |
| $  43.61 | North Rim Gift Shop, film, Café Diem sign, bookmark |
| $  20.00 | Group Workcamps (photo CD from camp) |
| $ 114.97 | Kits Camera (photos and CD) |
| $  36.64 | Kits Camera (reprints and enlargements) |
| $  12.55 | USPS (postage to mail photos) |
| $ 357.18 | total photos, Souvenirs, and attractions   *($400 budgeted)* |

## Lodging

| | |
|---|---|
| $  50.00 | First United Methodist Church of Boise—church check |
| $  50.00 | River of Life Christian Fellowship—church check |
| $  50.00 | Shepherd of the Hills United Methodist Church—church check |
| $ 150.00 | total lodging   *($200 budgeted)* |

## Workcamp

| | |
|---|---|
| $ 6,783.00 | tuition for 17 participants |
| $   150.00 | lost deposit for 3 unfilled spots |
| $ 6,933.00 | total workcamp cost   *($8,000 budgeted)* |

## Trip Totals

| | |
|---|---|
| $ 10,285.00 | budgeted   *($12,100 Budgeted – $1,815 for 3 participants)* |
| $ 10,404.36 | actual expenses |
| $   -119.36 | overage (due) |

# GROCERY LIST

| Item | Price | Item | Price |
|------|-------|------|-------|
| _____ | $_____ | _____ | $_____ |
| _____ | $_____ | _____ | $_____ |
| _____ | $_____ | _____ | $_____ |
| _____ | $_____ | _____ | $_____ |
| _____ | $_____ | _____ | $_____ |
| _____ | $_____ | _____ | $_____ |
| _____ | $_____ | _____ | $_____ |
| _____ | $_____ | _____ | $_____ |
| _____ | $_____ | _____ | $_____ |
| _____ | $_____ | _____ | $_____ |
| _____ | $_____ | _____ | $_____ |
| _____ | $_____ | _____ | $_____ |
| _____ | $_____ | _____ | $_____ |
| _____ | $_____ | _____ | $_____ |
| _____ | $_____ | _____ | $_____ |
| _____ | $_____ | _____ | $_____ |
| _____ | $_____ | _____ | $_____ |
| _____ | $_____ | _____ | $_____ |
| _____ | $_____ | _____ | $_____ |
| _____ | $_____ | _____ | $_____ |

# Sample Notary Form for International Travel With Minors

To Whom It May Concern:

I hereby give permission for my child, _____,
to participate in the Edmonds United Methodist Church Youth Group Mission Trip to Imuris Sonora, Mexico, from August 10 through August 19, 2002.

Furthermore, I hereby appoint Jason B. Schultz as a guardian of the above listed child and grant him guardianship power and authority to act in my behalf for the benefit of this child during the following period: August 10, 2002, through August 19, 2002.

And, whereas I have granted guardianship to Jason B. Schultz, I certify that it is allowable and appropriate for him to travel with my child outside the borders of the United States and into Mexico during the dates of August 10, through August 19, 2002.

Parent Name (Print): _____

Parent Signature: _____ Date: _____

STATE OF WASHINGTON
COUNTY OF _____

On this day personally appeared before me _____
_____, to me known to be the individual(s) described in and who executed the within and foregoing instrument, and acknowledged that he/she/they signed the same as his/her/their free and voluntary act and deed, for the uses and purposes therein mentioned.

Given under my hand and seal of office this _____ day of _____, 20_____.

Notary signature: _____
Printed name: _____
Notary Public residing at _____
My commission expires: _____

Youth Signature: _____ Date: _____
Jason B. Schultz: _____ Date: _____
   (Youth Director)

# PARENTAL CONSENT FORM

### Please print in ink.

Effective dates: ___ - ___ - ___ through ___ - ___ - ___

name _____
    last                    first                    middle

age _____ birthday _____

year in school _____        check one:  ☐ male   ☐ female

address _____

city _____ state _____ zip _____

phone _____ e-mail _____ pager / cell _____

medical insurance company _____ policy # _____

mother's name _____
    phone: home _____        work _____

father's name _____
    phone: home _____        work _____

emergency contact _____
    phone: home _____        work _____

physician _____        office phone _____

dentist _____        office phone _____

If necessary, describe in detail the nature and severity of any physical and/or psychological ailment, illness, propensity, weakness, limitation, handicap, disability, or condition to which your child is subject and of which the staff should be aware, and what (if any) action of protection is required on account thereof. Attach the notification to this form. Include names of medications and dosages that must be taken.

**Check the appropriate boxes. Attach another page with detail if necessary.**

1.  My child is a . . .  ☐ good swimmer        ☐ fair swimmer        ☐ non-swimmer

2. My child has allergies to . . .
   ☐ pollen    ☐ medications    ☐ food    ☐ insect bites or stings    ☐ other (list)

3. My child suffers from, has experienced, or is currently being treated for . . .
   ☐ asthma            ☐ epilepsy / seizure disorder        ☐ heart trouble
   ☐ diabetes          ☐ frequently upset stomach           ☐ physical handicap

4. Date of last tetanus shot: ___ - ___ - ___

5. My child wears        ☐ glasses        ☐ contact lenses

Please list and explain any major illnesses the child experienced during the last year.


   additional comments:

Should this child's activities be restricted for any reason? Please explain.


For your information, we expect each student to conform to these rules of conduct:
   • No possession or use of alcohol, drugs, or tobacco
   • No students driving
   • No fighting, weapons, fireworks, lighters, or explosives
   • No offensive or immodest clothing
   • No boys in girls' sleeping quarters and no girls in boys' sleeping quarters
   • Participation in group activities
   • Respect for property
   • Respect group members, staff, and adult leaders
   • Respect and compliance with event schedules

   Students who fail to comply with these expectations may be sent home at their
   parents' expense.

I have read the rules of conduct, the above evaluation of my health, and permission to
participate in youth group activities. I agree to abide by the stated personal limitations and
code of conduct.

Student signature: _____ Date: ___ - ___ - ___

(Name of student) _____

has my permission to attend all youth activities sponsored by (church name)

_____ from

___ - ___ - ___ to ___ - ___ - ___. This consent form gives permission to seek whatever medical attention is deemed necessary and releases the Church and its staff of any liability against personal losses of the named child.

I/We, the undersigned, have legal custody of the student named above, a minor, and have given our consent for him/her to attend events being organized by the Church. I/We understand that there are inherent risks involved in any ministry or athletic event, and I/we hereby release the Church, its pastors, employees, agents, and volunteer workers from any and all liability for any injury, loss, or damage to person or property that may occur during the course of my/our child's involvement.

In the event that he/she is injured and requires the attention of a doctor, I/we consent to any reasonable medical treatment as deemed necessary by a licensed physician. In the event that treatment is required from a physician and/or hospital-staff member designated by the Church, I/we agree to hold such person free from any claims, demands, or suits for damages arising from the giving of such consent. I/We also acknowledge that we will be ultimately responsible for the cost of any medical care should the cost of that medical care not be reimbursed by the health insurance provider.

Further, I/we affirm that the health insurance information provided on page 1 is accurate at this date and will, to the best of my/our knowledge, still be in force for the student during the specified dates above. I/we also agree to bring my/our child home at my/our own expense should he/she become ill or if the student ministries staff member deems the measure necessary.

Parent/guardian signature:

_____

Date ___ - ___ - ___

# MISSION PLANNING TIMELINE

## For a Summer Mission

**September–October:** Brainstorm and decide on project.

**October–November:** Make arrangements and secure dates.

**November–December:** Publicize, and recruit participants (youth and adult).

**December–May:** Fundraising, pre-trip training, finalizing arrangements

**June:** Prep for departure

**July:** Mission

**August–September:** Follow up and follow through.

**September—October:** Brainstorm, and decide on a new project.

## For a Spring-Break Mission

**May–June:** Start planning for next year's trip.

**July–September:** Secure the dates, and arrange logistics.

**September:** Begin publicity and sign-ups.

**October–February:** Do fundraising and pre-trip training and preparation.

**February–March:** Prepare for departure.

**March–April:** Do the mission.

**May:** Start planning next year's mission.

## General Guidelines

If you are going year to year without planning ahead, plan early so that you can get a good start on your mission experience.

Looking ahead and planning out a two-, three-, or four-year strategy will help you develop an ongoing missions ministry. Youth workers can have difficulty to planning far ahead because of the constant turnover that comes with graduation. Juniors and seniors aren't going to be on the missions three and four years down the road, and younger youth might not want to do what someone else planned. Try to find a balance of planning ahead while providing a way for youth who will be participating to have a say.

If your group goes to the same location every year, planning out a three- to four-year strategy may not be as vital for a group that changes locations or projects each year.

## An Example of Looking Ahead Three to Four Years

**This year:** a local, less expensive mission

**Next year:** a "bigger" mission away but still in the US

**Two years from now:** a local, less expensive mission

**Three years out:** an international mission

# Insta-Mission Organizations

**Note:** The websites and resources listed are current as of READY-TO-GO MISSIONS publication date. The mission organizations and resources are recommendations from the author and are not necessarily endorsed by Abingdon Press.

**Adventures in Missions**
*adventures.org*
1-800-881-2461

**Appalachia Service Project**
*asphome.org*
(423) 854-8800

**Christian Appalachian Project**
*www.chrisapp.org*
1-800-755-5322

**Christian Outreach International**
*coiusa.com*
1-800-451-3643

**Christ in Youth**
*ciy.com*
(417) 781-2273

**Crop Walk**
*churchworldservice.org/CROP/*
1-888-CWS-CROP

**EPIC Adventures**
*epicadventures.org*
1-800-264-5129

**Footsteps Missions**
*footstepsmissions.org*
(650) 327-1703

**Group Workcamps Foundation**
*groupworkcamps.com*
1-800-385-4545

**Heifer International**
*www.heifer.org*

**International Family Missions**
*ifmus.org*
(303) 665-7635

**LeaderTreks**
*leadertreks.com*
1-877-502-0699

**Mission Discovery**
*missiondiscovery.org*
1-800-767-8720

**Mountain T.O.P. (Tennessee Outreach Project)**
*mountain-top.org*
(931) 692-3999

**Pacific Northwest Cross Connection**
*pncc.info*

**Sierra Service Project**
*sierraserviceproject.org*
(916) 488-6441

**OC International**
*www.onechallenge.org*
1-800-676-7837

**STEM Ministries**
*stemintl.org*
1-877-STEM-646